JANE AUSTEN AND MARY SHELLEY AND THEIR SISTERS

..ited by

Laura Dabundo

University Press of America,® Inc.
Lanham • New York • Oxford

Copyright 2000 by
University Press of America, ® Inc.
4720 Boston Way
Lanham, Maryland 20706

12 Hid's Copse Rd.
Cumnor Hill, Oxford OX2 9JJ

British Library Cataloging in Publication Information Available

Library of Congress Cataloging-in-Publication Data

Jane Austen and Mary Shelley, and their sisters / edited by Laura Dabando.
p.   cm.
Includes bibliographical references and index.
l. English fiction—Women authors—History and criticism. 2. Women and
literature—Great Britain—History—19th century. 3. Shelley, Mary
Wollstonecraft, 1797-1851—Criticism and interpretation. 4. Austen, Jane,
1775-1817—Criticism and interpretation. 5. English fiction—19th century—
History and criticism. I. Dabando, Laura. I. Title.
PR868.W6J36   2000   —dc21   99-087446 CIP

ISBN 0-7618-1611-9 (cloth: alk. ppr.)
ISBN 0-7618-1612-7 (pbk: alk. ppr.)

♾™ The paper used in this publication meets the minimum
requirements of American National Standard for Information
Sciences—Permanence of Paper for Printed Library Materials,
ANSI Z39.48—1984

For my father, Leonard Nicholas Dabundo

Without any display of doing more than the rest, or any fear of doing too much, he was always true to her interests, and considerate of her feelings, trying to make her good qualities understood, and to conquer the diffidence which prevented their being more apparent; giving her advice, consolation, and encouragement.

Jane Austen, *Mansfield Park*

Acknowledgements

This book has been a joy on which to work and from which to learn. I am grateful to the authors of the essays for their collegiality, their contributions, and their restraint and patience during the seemingly interminable course of this project. Thanks are also due to my secretaries extraordinaire at Kennesaw State University, Darlene Luke and Shirley Dean, who have kept me organized and on track and have set a superlative standard for the smooth execution of duty with a minimum of fuss and feathers. Above all, I am indebted to the yeoman labors of Deborah Whitehurst to prepare camera-ready copy and to incorporate endless corrections, with unfailing grace, care, promptitude, and professionalism. Last, I could not have produced this work in any form without the support and encouragement of my colleagues and friends in the Department of English and elsewhere across campus here at one of Georgia's finest. Thanks and blessings upon all, and may we all dwell in the beneficent community that Jane Austen bestows upon the Knightley-Woodhouse clan at the end of *Emma*, recognized and beatified as "the small band of true friends," mutually sustained and enriched in comity, amity, and peace.

Contents

Introduction

While thus far there are estimable collections of criticism on Mary Shelley and on Jane Austen and useful compendia of biographical data on many less widely known women novelists of the Romantic age, *Jane Austen and Mary Shelley and Their Sisters* is an inaugural volume to consider Shelley and Austen in the very context they themselves would have recognized as theirs (English fiction by women during the 1780s to the 1830s). Also, this is one of the first books to consider seriously the literary achievements of many less known writers. In other words, very simply, on both fronts, this book attempts to define the field of women novelists of the Romantic period, a field for a long time exclusively designated as the province of male poets. Recognizing the limitations of that, scholars have been rediscovering poetry by women and expanding the poetic canon, and the literary canon for the period in general is enlarging. Truly it is time, then, to define the field of novels by women during this season.

Back in the days before William Blake was nudged into the poetic canon by Northrop Frye and Harold Bloom (starting in the 1950s), Sir Walter Scott ranked with Wordsworth, Coleridge, Shelley, Keats, and Byron as the period's worthies, and his lordship's eminence seemed securely anchored on two foundations: his poetry and his fiction. However, Blake's emergence seems to have been the proximate blow that dislodged Scott poetically, and the speed with which Scott catapulted from grace was sufficient to displace novelistic purchase as well. Protracted historical novels were no longer *au courant* anyway. In fact, the result, if not the intent, was a very tidy entirely poetic cast to the Romantic Age.

Furthering that end, in fact, were successful efforts to dismiss Mary Shelley's *Frankenstein* as either the ill-written nightmare of a teenaged girl or the pseudonymous ravings of Percy and to leave forgotten the rest of her works, along with the multitudes of other novels, including dozens upon dozens written by women of the period.

Jane Austen, though clearly writing and publishing in the Romantic period--however anyone calibrates that disputed chronology--was either dropped entirely into the apparent void lacking notable fiction opened between the eighteenth century and the Victorian novels or relegated to the dustbins of unimportant women's fiction (for if not by) or mere time-passing novels of manners or, most commonly perhaps, eased into the final flourish of Neoclassicism on the basis of superficial readings of her work. However, the truth is otherwise as scholars of the last generation are demonstrating.

England and America both in the early years of the nineteenth century were overwhelmed with what Hawthorne spitefully tried to discount as "that damned mob of scribbling women." Vast amounts of poetry and fiction were spilling from women's pens. Just consult the chronology included in this volume for a representative sampling of this deluge (arbitrarily holding the flood-gates at 1783 and 1840). And note, too, the curiosities that it reveals. Consider, for example, the year 1816, when both Jane Austen's elegantly planned and perfected, if quietly received, novel *Emma* and Caroline Lamb's disorderly, public, and anti-Byronic *roman e clef Glenarvon* come to light simultaneously with the more conventional and didactic *Valentine's Eve* by Amelia Opie and the posthumous work of the immensely acclaimed Agnes Maria Bennett, ominously titled *Faith and Fiction, or Shining Lights in a Dark Generation.* Compare two years later, when Austen's Gothic satire *Northanger Abbey* apparently sounds the death knell for that genre at the same time that its lifeblood, as it were, receives a revivifying transfusion with the great Romantic tour de force *Frankenstein.* Readers that year, too, bought up copies of more earnestly grounded works, such as Sydney Owenson's satiric and sentimental Irish *Florence McCarthy* as well as Susan Ferrier's Scottish moralizing but amiable *Marriage.* Moreover, the year is marked by the publication of Mary Martha Sherwood's most famous work (*A History of the Fairchild Family, or The Child's Manual*), characterized by a preachy spirit similar to that of Ferrier's, along with the historical confection of Anna Maria Porter, *The Fast of St. Magdalen.* And these two particular years, which I single out here simply because they feature works by the two established women writers we remember, are not atypical for what else they demonstrate, as we see. Clearly, women were not writing to a formula but were responding to an insatiable market for their infinitely varied wares. And the still adolescent form of the developing genre of the novel was proving most accommodating in its elasticity and capaciousness. So how are we, then, to take this field in a direction that will yield delineation, description, and, ultimately perhaps, definition?

This book offers a variegated selection of essays extending to nearly fifteen women novelists of the Romantic period whose works encompass the prevailing realities of politics, religion, the Gothic, psychology, literature, sociology, philosophy, pedagogy, feminism, the theater, science, and adventure, among other categories, which are just the terms of these fourteen essays. Indeed, the diversity of approaches and subjects here epitomizes the period's wealth, to which the book's chronology of novels by women writers in England at the time amply testifies. Here, at last, Wollstonecraft, Edgeworth, Burney, Austen, and Shelley stand among their sisters.

And what their diversity itself registers is the elasticity, the flexibility of the newly emergent, increasingly dominant genre of extended prose fiction. Here, at last, is a form conducive to innovation and tradition; accommodating to individual vagaries of style and substance; and hospitable to a range of characters, plots, and settings marking off a continuum of reasonable and passionate behavior, an expressive form that women of sundry backgrounds, inclinations, and interests could utilize, mold, and make their own. In some way, the novel answers at least some of the needs of these fifteen women writers and all their sisters.

What is apparent from even a cursory survey of this period is that in a time when women are excluded from power, property, dominion, and authority, literary expression opens up a single avenue of opportunity for talent to speak, for intelligence to shine, for imagination to sparkle. And what the novelists in particular do, as these essays demonstrate, I believe, is not craft escapist fantasies taking them and their readers far distant from the harsh realities of the last quarter of the eighteenth and first third of the nineteenth centuries but rather to undertake skillful, articulate, and energetic encounters, skirmishes, at times terrorist attacks if not outright warfare with the prevailing, established customs, institutions, and verities. That is to say, these essays chart the dialogue in which these women engage with the documents and forms of their society and culture. Thus we find Radcliffe linked with educational treatises and practices; Burney, Williams, Edgeworth, Shelley, and Wollstonecraft confronting propaganda, mindsets, and political agendas; Shelley in the context of the traditions of the theater of the day; Ferrier sparring with the lordly Milton's texts; women writers playing against the grain of received conventions; Austen exploiting fledgling aesthetic Romanticism; Smith and many of the others raising feminist strains to counter settled patriarchal expectations. These women do not speak in one voice; their subversion, as is often the case among the dispossessed, is not even harmonized; it is a chorus we hear, a cacophony perhaps, but a thrilling, stirring opera with the establishment. The age of Romanticism was highly politicized and self-conscious. Need we be surprised that the fiction by women participates in that? The riches of the time are the riches of these works.

Responding to the French Revolution: Williams's *Julia* and Burney's *The Wanderer*

Deborah Kennedy

Helen Maria Williams's first and only novel, *Julia* (1790), written during the early months of the French Revolution, and Frances Burney's last novel, *The Wanderer; or, Female Difficulties* (1814), span twenty-five years of British response to revolutionary activity in France. Williams, a young radical, and Burney, a mature woman with experience enough of "female difficulties," both make use of the historical opportunity of the Revolution to critique society and gender relations. In the context of 1814, *The Wanderer* is a more radical book than *Julia* appears to its 1790 audience. Burney's novel enters a conservative world, as a long and troubled work that sits uncomfortably next to the genteel volumes of Jane Austen, and provides a Cassandra-like answer to Williams's hopes for the future.

The plot of *Julia* addresses a love triangle that immediately places the story in relationship to popular eighteenth-century works such as *The Sorrows of Young Werther, The New Eloise,* and *Sir Charles Grandison*. The plain but sweet Charlotte Clifford brings her fiancé Frederick Seymour home, and he proceeds to fall in love with her beautiful cousin Julia. Frederick confesses his love to Julia but marries Charlotte, who is devastated when she learns that Frederick does not love her. The year passes, with all three agonized by their various feelings of desire, guilt, and betrayal. Charlotte soon gives birth to a son, but Seymour dies, pledging his love to Julia.

The dearest evidence of the novel's prorevolutionary bias has nothing to do with the main plot. It is in a poem celebrating the fall of the Bastille--a poem that is actually a vision of the future, since the novel is set in 1776. Specifying the year of the American *Declaration of Independence,* Williams connects the two revolutions as part of one struggle for the improvement of the human condition. Julia's suitor, the admirable Mr. F--, receives the prophetic poem on the Bastille from an English friend just released from that prison. Previously Mr. F-- tells Julia about his brother fighting in America, a story much like Williams's earlier antiwar poem "An American Tale" (1786). Using Mr. F--, a male intermediary, to introduce the political material into the novel, Williams avoids directly involving her heroines in politics, but later in 1790 she does involve herself by publishing the first volume of her *Letters from France,* which initiates a career devoted "almost entirely to sketches of the event of the Revolution" (*Poems* ix).

It is important to consider whether or not the only political or revolutionary presence in *Julia* is these anomalous anecdotes of Mr. F--. Although her biographer Lionel Woodward says of the novel, "She is above all influenced by the French revolution, and one notices in this novel that democratic and levelling spirit that will characterize her later works" (207; my translation), M. Ray Adams finds "little or no hint of the revolutionary ferment" in it (98). Apart from the materials introduced by the progressive Mr. F--, Williams focuses almost exclusively on the love triangle, and the reader finds herself in the very closed world of the Clifford and Seymour families. Yet the subject of marriage involves the public and private spheres and is considered germane to the Revolution according to one review of a French book on divorce published in 1789:

> It was to be expected that among the various corrections and improvements projected by the French nation, in the present era of revolution and change, we should find some new regulations respecting marriage; one of the most interesting and important objects that can fall under the cognisance of a legislature. (Rev. of *Du Divorce*)

In the late eighteenth century, several women writers raise the issue of divorce, even if only by implication, when they draw attention to bad marriages, as in the notable examples of Mary Wollstonecraft's Maria in *The Wrongs of Woman,* Charlotte Smith's Lady Adelina in *Emmeline,* and Geraldine Verney in *Desmond.* Although their arguments rest on the fact that these worthy women are tied to brutal husbands, Williams is interested in good people whose affections are mismatched.

Julia and Charlotte are both exemplary young women of feeling whose benevolence sets them apart from the selfish and superficial women of their acquaintance. Williams does not urge the reader to choose between them, but describes their respective positions as the abandoned woman (Charlotte is abandoned in emotional terms) and the "other" woman. Nonetheless, despite Charlotte's worthiness, Julia is clearly the more suitable partner for Frederick because of their intellectual compatibility, something for which Williams argues when she exposes Julia's jealousy:

> Julia, whose understanding was far superior to Charlotte's, soon perceived that the powers of Seymour's mind were not fully discerned by her cousin; that often a stroke of wit, an emanation of fancy, which she herself admired, was not comprehended by Charlotte; and that a mind less superior to the general mass of mankind would have made her happy. (1:113)

It is a delicate task for Williams to show the differences between the two women, without deprecating Charlotte, who is "everything the heart can wish in a domestic companion" (1:227), which, while complimentary, also ascribes to her a conventionality that Julia, to her credit it seems, lacks.

Wollstonecraft's review of the novel complains that Julia is too good to be true, "a rock against which the waves vainly beat" (Rev. 99), implying that Julia does not at all respond to Frederick's overtures. But Wollstonecraft must have missed the subtle indications of Julia's sexual arousal in, not only her blushes, but her response to nature and her physical interactions. In one incident, after an agonizing talk with Seymour, Julia returns to her room, gazing out the window at the "dark rocks" and the flashing northern lights, their motion "stronger than usual" (1:230). Earlier, when visiting some distant ruins, her responses clearly differentiate her from her cousin:

> The wind had risen, and the lake was violently agitated: Julia turned her eyes from the abbey, to contemplate the surges of the lake, while Charlotte, who was at a little distance behind, leaning on Seymour, stopped to look at a cavity in the wall, in which the snail had made his nest. (1:196)

Julia's attraction to the agitated lake conveys her passion, while Charlotte's interest in the snail in the wall reinforces her identity as an archetypal domestic woman, who leans dependently on her fiancé. After Julia is injured by a rock fall, she has to lean on Seymour while Charlotte goes for help. This particular episode is the first of two dangerous physical encounters that not only seem to displace Julia's passion but also act as a substitute for sexual intimacy with Frederick.

The second encounter is part of a series of events building with intensity toward the end of the novel. After having a nightmare about Charlotte, Julia finds Seymour downstairs where they look at prints illustrating Goethe's *Werther*. Against Julia's objections, he defends Werther's suicide as a remedy for "the heart that is bleeding with an incurable wound" (2:202). Later that day, in the wake of their quasi-sexual conversation, Julia leaves a supper party because of a bad headache, and when a chair breaks, "her forehead [is] cut with broken glass" and bleeds violently (2:207). She sustains a physical injury that corresponds to Seymour's figurative bleeding and wounded heart, and her body undergoes a trauma that refigures sexual intercourse and is followed by a ride home with Seymour--in Charlotte's carriage (2:207). Later, when he is on his deathbed, he shows no remorse about loving Julia and tells her, "how often have I desired that you might be near me when I yielded my last breath" (2:236). Julia lets him kiss her hand and mixes "her tears with his" (2:233), a sexual moment that concludes their chaste affair.

While Williams advocates self-control in the advertisement and elsewhere in the book, the novel exposes the problem of transferred and transgressive affection without providing pat solutions to this very realistic dilemma. Setting out to show "the danger arising from the uncontrolled indulgence of strong affections" that can involve "even the virtuous in calamity" (I:iii), Williams at the same time implies that the codes of honor that require a man to marry his fiancé even though he loves someone else or to stay married when love is not there result in sorrow and agony for all concerned. She shows that love cannot be reasoned: Frederick cannot convince himself to love Charlotte, and Julia cannot convince herself to marry Mr. F--. Like Richardson's Clementina and Harriet, Julia cannot marry where she does not love (Richardson 4:404, 7:391).

By privileging the right of individual choice in love, Williams looks beyond the private sphere to question duty to moral codes. In the midst of the final intense scenes, she introduces the poem about the fall of the Bastille, which seems especially relevant in light of Tony Tanner's assessment that in the bourgeois novel "the action of adultery portends the possible breakdown of all the mediations on which society itself depends" (17). Drawing on conventional imagery of the Bastille, Williams combines a sentimental description of the English prisoner, a horrifying story of his dream of the legendary Man in the Iron Mask, and a tribute to the glorious future for the "millions with according mind/Who claim the rights of human kind" (2:221)--prisoners and peasants whose lives will be shaped by the power of enlightened philosophy to "renovate the gladdened earth" (2:223). Although the images of imprisonment and freedom can be read as projections of Julia and Frederick's desire, equally telling is the reference on the next page to Charlotte's "confinement" (2:224). Williams never ignores Charlotte's role as the rejected woman, depicting it sympathetically and convincingly (see 2:125-142).

The Bastille falls, accompanied by celebrations for the future freedom of humankind, and Williams's characters find new freedoms: Frederick dies, allowing Charlotte and Julia to be best friends again, and Mrs. Meynell joins them after her own troublesome husband dies of fever in India. The three women live together peacefully; they have money, rooms of their own, and a male protector in Mr. Clifford. Julia remains single, refusing many "honourable offers of marriage" (2:245), an ending that seems to confirm Williams's sympathy for transgressive love because Julia is faithful to the memory of Frederick, her "one unconquered weakness" (2:245). As Eleanor Ty notes, "Williams is asserting the possibility of a woman's attaining a position as full subject without being married or becoming the specularized 'other' of a man" (79). It is as if traditional domestic arrangements resemble the "hated walls" and "threatening towers" (2:221) of the Bastille itself, an association rendered by Wollstonecraft's Maria: "Marriage had bastilled me" (Wollstonecraft 155). Taking an opposing point of view, one critic senses something is wrong when, in an otherwise favorable review, he or she objects to Julia receiving "the punishment of celibacy" (Rev. of *Julia* 593). However, rather than punishing Julia, Williams rewards her with the gift of independence, a lesson learned from the American and French Revolutions and applied here to women's lives.

Frances Burney's last novel, set in England during the period of the Reign of Terror, follows the wanderings of Miss Ellis--a kind of "princess in disguise" (75, 110, 523)--who is fleeing France. The turbulent times offer an appropriate background for a novel that, though it has little to do with activities in France and much to do with the heroine's English social and economic circumstances, is an ambitious and daring work, arguably Burney's most feminist. *The Wanderer* is a conservative fairy tale, complicated by its realistic examination of questions of women's rights and women's work and by its portrayal of the character Elinor Joddrel, who is modeled on Wollstonecraft.

Burney's own life was completely changed by the French Revolution, since she met her husband Alexandre D'Arblay when he resided in

Mickleham with other French emigrants. Burney began writing *The Wanderer* around 1798 (Doody 286), continued working on it during her ten-year residence in France, and had three of the five volumes completed by the time she returned to England in August, 1812. Although Burney's novel falls on the antijacobin side of the debate, it is decidedly not anti-French. She condemns the Revolution, but she is sympathetic to the emigrants and ridicules English ignorance about France. It is foolish Mr. Scope who says, "I have no very high notion, I own, of the morals of those foreigners at this period" (79), just as in Charlotte Smith's *The Banished Man* (1794) the ignorant dandy Melton scorns the novel's hero D'Alonville, a French emigrant, by lumping all French together: "Frenchmen--Jacobins--Sans Culottes--whatever they are pleased to call themselves" (Smith 3:6 1). Because of what Peter Hughes calls "an attack on the illiberalism of the British towards foreigners" (Burney, *Journals* 8:318 n.), *The Wanderer* seems unpatriotic to at least one critic who complains that "her long residence in France has given Madame D'Arblay a very novel and surprising view of the state of religion, manners, and society in England" (Rev. of *The Wanderer* 128). Burney reacted to the "harsh treatment" given to her "poor Wanderer" (Burney, *Journals* 8:317) by hoping that this youngest child" "may share, in a few years, the partiality shewn to its Elder sisters" (Burney, *Journals* 8:317). It has taken more than a few years, but the novel is now in print again, and Anne Mellor has recently called it Burney's best (83).

The Wanderer opens in medias res, with a small boatload of English people about to return from France. The main character, Juliet, joins the passengers at the last minute, disguised and secretive. Known throughout most of the novel as the enigmatic Miss Ellis, she is an aristocratic English woman raised in France, who is escaping a brutal French Commissary who forced her into marriage in order to collect her portion of 6,000 pounds. Although her traveling companions will be safe once they land in England, Juliet's anxieties continue because she agreed to marry the Commissary only to prevent him from executing her friend the Bishop, and until she is sure of his safety she cannot approach her family in England to claim her right as the eldest daughter from the deceased Lord Granville's first but secret marriage.

Juliet's problems are only partly due to the "dire reign of the terrific Robespierre" (11). If her father had openly acknowledged his marriage to the poor but virtuous Miss Powell in the first place, then his daughter Juliet would have been brought up with the children of his second marriage, Aurora and Lord Melbury. Instead, he was afraid to stand up to his own father, so he had Juliet raised in France and died before he had a chance to acknowledge her formally. Since it is her father's cowardice that causes Juliet some of her "difficulties," the reader can see where the revolutionary concept of defying custom could have been honorably applied in this case. However, Juliet's maternal uncle, Admiral Powell, argues against unequal marriages:

> My sister did but a foolish thing, after all, in marrying that young lord...You would never have been smuggled out of your native land, in that fashion, if she had taken up with a man in her own rank of life...see the difference of those topsy-turvey marriages!--a worthy tar would have been proud of my sister for his wife; while your lord was only ashamed of her! (843)

Ending a chapter with this speech, Burney debates the issue of "topsy-turvey marriages": Is Miss Powell foolish to marry a young Lord-- should that revolutionary action be resisted, despite the success of Richardson's Pamela? Or does the elegant and accomplished Juliet prove that good can come from such a union?

Juliet's own marriage shows another instance of class crossing since the Commissary would never have had access to an empowering promissory note or been able to threaten her into marrying him without his position of authority as Robespierre's officer. Although the brutal character of the Commissary is the main vehicle for Burney to attack the French Revolutionaries, the relationship exemplifies the more general situation in which women are subject to the men who determine their position in and out of marriage. The Commissary marries Julia to get her legacy, and Lord Denmeath--Lord Granville's brother-in-law by his second wife--is eager to sell her for that price so that she will not claim her proper inheritance. Moreover, Juliet enacts an extreme but not atypical female sacrifice by marrying because of her inordinate duty to another patriarch, the elderly Bishop who raised her.

Burney's noted fascination with naming, a subject explored by Margaret Anne Doody and subsequent critics, is crucial to *The Wanderer* because Juliet's identity is in a state of suspension. She is not publicly known as Lord Granville's eldest daughter, and she cannot literally claim that name if she is legally married to the French Commissary. The reader does not discover Miss Ellis's true name until halfway through the novel, and we never know her married name because the Commissary remains undistinguished. The act of naming takes on special significance in the French Revolution when hereditary nobility and titles were abolished by the decree of June 19, 1790. Many people lost the name they were accustomed to using; the appellations "citoyen" and "citoyenne" were common; and the familiar "tu" replaced the formal "vous." Burney emphasizes the existential crisis resulting from name changing when Juliet asks: "O when may I cast off this veil of humiliating concealment? when meet unappalled the fair eye of open day? when appear,--when alas!--even know what I am!" (673).

Juliet's husband is known only by his job title, which seems a comment on the dehumanizing bureaucracy of the Jacobin government. His character is unequivocally brutal, like that of his leader, who is variously denominated as "Mr. Robertspierre," "Mounseer Robert Speer," and "Bob Speer" (79, 93, 257, 466). Following conventional portraits of Jacobins from Burke onward, Burney makes the Commissary into a monstrous force of masculine aggression. In 1792, the royalist J. Peltier published *The Late Picture of Paris,* an example of the fiercest antijacobin rhetoric, which advocates exterminating "this new race of ferocious animals" (437), a phrase reminiscent of the later nameless monster in Frankenstein, whose connection to the French Revolution has been analyzed by Sterrenburg. The Commissary is "large made, tall and strong" (727), has an "air of ferocious authority," walks with "large strides" (726), dresses "with disgusting negligence," and presents "an hideous countenance" (726). Their marriage is unconsummated, and when he finds Juliet in England he treats her in a way that augurs rape: he "roughly seized her arm, with one hand, while, with the other, he rudely lifted up her bonnet" (726). Finally, after his arrest, he leaves, "storming, raging, and swearing, his face distorted with fury, his under-jaw dropt, and his mouth foaming" (734). Burney's own "Fearful" encounters with two French police officers in Dunkirk in 1812 could easily have supplied a prototype for Juliet's husband. In a long journal entry, Burney recounts her interrogation by the "Tyger," whose "air of dreadful menace" accompanies "a Voice of Thunder" (Burney, *Journals* 6:723, 721,722); earlier another officer at the Dunkirk customs office reacts "with fire and fury" when he sees she is trying to transport a manuscript (*The Wanderer,* as it turned out): "he sputtered at the Mouth, & stamped with his feet, so forcibly & vociferously" (Burney, *Journals* 6:716).

The physical monstrosity of the Commissary is also attributed to the otherwise genteel Elinor Joddrel when she fervently espouses the revolutionary cause. Elinor's appearance is never described except when she looks unwomanly and dangerous: "The eyes of Elinor were wild and fierce, her complexion was livid, her countenance was become haggard" (172) and later: "Elinor appeared in deep mourning; her long hair, wholly unornamented, hanging loosely down her shoulders. Her complexion was wan, her eyes were fierce rather than bright, and her air was wild and menacing" (359). Although her appearance and behavior seem out of control, that befits irrational revolutionaries; what Elinor says about politics is in keeping with the rational and sympathetic responses of early supporters of the Revolution in the period before the execution of the King, the fall of the Girondins, and the escalation of the Reign of Terror. She embodies the initial optimism and the hope for a change that would emancipate not just the French but all humankind:

> The grand effect...of beholding so many millions of men let loose from all ties, divine or human, gave such play to my fancy, such a range to my thoughts, and brought forth such new, unexpected, and untried combinations to my reason, that I frequently felt as if just created, and ushered into the world. (156)

An apocalyptic change was broadly proclaimed, as in this comment by Richard Price from "A Discourse on the Love of Our Country" (1789): "I have lived to see thirty millions of people, indignant and resolute, spurning at slavery, and demanding liberty with an irresistible voice" (195). Many supporters of the early phase of the Revolution excused the violence, as Williams does in 1792:

> And shall we, because the fanatics of liberty have committed some detes-table crimes, conclude that liberty is an evil and prefer the gloomy tran-quillity of despotism?...Men have been long treated with inhumanity, therefore they are ferocious...But the genuine principles of enlightened freedom will soon be better comprehended and may perhaps at no distant period be adopted by all the nations of Europe. (*Letters from France* 1.2.204-205)

Williams and many others who could forgive in 1792 are sickened by the end of 1793, and only committed Jacobins like the English writer Sampson Perry express virtually unqualified support at that stage of the Revolution. For example, Williams's reactions upon being released from prison in Paris in December, 1793, are very different from Elinor's. Walking outside of the city to get away from Paris, "that den of carnage, that slaughterhouse of man," Williams is troubled to see members of the revolutionary jury enjoying a ramble in the park, "steeped as they were to the very lips in blood" (*Letters from France* 2.2.3-4). Elinor, on the other hand, upon returning from Paris in

December, 1793, claims that: "those excesses are only the first froth of the cauldron. When once 'tis skimmed, you will find the composition clear, sparkling, delicious" (18). Although the sentiment compares with those of 1792, the imagery is grossly inappropriate for 1793, for no one in France during the Reign of Terror can innocently refer to drinking something out of a "cauldron." The word itself bears negative connotations from *Macbeth,* associating Elinor with Shakespeare's witches, but more pertinently, since the sight of blood is universal with the increase in executions, the statement also conjures images of drinking blood, something commonly depicted in caricatures and stories about Jacobins and their victims (Hibbert 175). At the end of the novel, a short speech by Harleigh provides the final comment on the Revolution and exhibits a sense of distance and objectivity more in keeping with the perspective of a date later than July, 1794. Harleigh reflects rather too tamely upon the "individuals who have borne in it any share, and who, according to their temperaments and dispositions, have received its new doctrines as lessons or as warnings" (869). Surely a man who has several months before been released from a French prison, recently been harassed by a woman styling herself on the Republican suicides, and only days before watched his sweetheart being dragged off by a rough French Jacobin would speak more strongly about the horrors of the Revolution. Harleigh's speech sounds more like the response of a later historian than a witness of the Revolution.

Despite the anachronistic tendencies of Burney's characterization, Elinor eloquently defends her support for the rights of men and of women, but, tragically, she finds no useful sphere of action for promoting her cause. Though she condemns "men--who would keep us from every office, but making puddings and pies" (399), she can find no "office" for herself except choosing her marriage partner, which means aggressively courting Albert Harleigh rather than waiting for him to court her--something disapproved of by even the liberated William Godwin who describes his courtship with Wollstonecraft as "one sex did not take the priority which long-established custom has awarded it, nor the other overstep that delicacy which is so severely imposed" (257). Elinor does "overstep that delicacy" since her obsession with Harleigh consumes all of her energy, and as Judy Sims notes she is "subject to uncontrolled emotionalism and as dependent on masculine approval as her meeker sisters" (109). Attempting suicide twice, Elinor not only acts more like a female Werther than a Republican, but also resembles Wollstonecraft who twice tried to kill herself when Gilbert Imlay ended their affair, incidents that become public knowledge when Godwin publishes the *Memoirs* in 1798. Wollstonecraft's "burning imagination" and "delusive visions" (247, 253) are also Elinor's. The historical woman and the fictional one are both more memorable for their illicit passion than their intellectual accomplishments, a fact that Elinor, at least, jokes about: "If I were poor myself, I would engage to acquire a large fortune, in less than a week, by advertising, at two-pence a head, a sight of the lady that stabbed herself" (400).

Elinor's failed and unfeminine courting of Harleigh makes a mockery out of her Republican sentiments, despite her stated attempt to find liberty by "throwing off the trammels of unmeaning custom, and acting, as well as thinking, for myself" (151). At the end of the novel, she muses on her status and her identity, asking of herself, as if she were a character in an historical drama, "must even Elinor. . .find that she has strayed from the beaten road, only to discover that all others are pathless!" (873). Burney, ambiguously sympathetic to Elinor, does not have her answer this question, thus allowing readers to ponder whether one "beaten road" is enough for women or if they should be able to choose from more.

Meanwhile, the heroine of the novel, frequently referred to as the "Incognita" and the "Wanderer," explores firsthand the paths open to women in the early 1790s. Because her money is stolen on the way over from France, Juliet arrives in England penniless and nameless. Her disguise as an old black woman emblematizes her marginalization. Once she removes the plasters and paint, her beauty and elegance gain her entry to the house of Mrs. Maple, and she makes use of her many accomplishments--music, drama, reading, drawing. But her secrecy makes her suspect, and Miss Ellis must constantly struggle to pay for her lodging, her clothes, her debts, and her transportation. On several occasions Juliet laments the "FEMALE DIFFICULTIES" which provide a practical counterpart to the philosophical concerns expressed in Elinor's speeches about that other capitalized term, "RIGHTS OF WOMAN." Revolutionary indeed is Burney's complex depiction of the lot of woman in this novel (see Epstein 191), as Miss Ellis wanders from "the stately homes of England" to the "cottage homes of England" (Hemans). In her efforts to earn money she also discovers that the rich treat the working class with a "total absence of feeling and of equity" (427). Despite her sympathy for the working poor, Juliet disdains their lack of refinement, demonstrating Burney insists on class distinctions when Miss Ellis ends up back where she belongs as Lady Juliet

Granville.

But the ending is uneasy, for both Juliet and Elinor have undergone radical--unladylike--experiences: Juliet marries a raving Jacobin, she sees the "ghastly bleeding head of a victim" of the guillotine (743), and her hand is "besmeared with blood" when she accidentally touches the contents of a poacher's basket (683); Elinor "plunged a dagger in her breast" ("the blood gushed out in torrents") (359), shoots a pistol, and disguises herself as a male emigrant. The events and ideas in this large novel are exciting and unsettling and fit a traditional, if limited definition of the term "romantic" in a way that the canonized, seemingly more sedate works of Austen do not. When Burney published this novel of the Revolution in 1814, Williams, who had forged a career writing nonfictional accounts of life in Revolutionary France, had been forced by Napoleon into silence and returned to more traditional literary work as a translator. If Williams read *The Wanderer,* she may have agreed with Burney that the Age of Revolution had provided the opportunity to examine but had done little to solve "female difficulties."

Works Cited

Adams, M. Ray. "Helen Maria Williams and the French Revolution." *Wordsworth and Coleridge.* Ed. Earl Leslie Griggs. New York: Russell, 1967. 87-117.

Burney, Fanny. *The Journal and Letters of Fanny Burney.* Ed. Joyce Hemlow. Vol.6. Oxford: Clarendon Press, 1975.

___. *The Journals and Letters of Fanny Burney.* Ed. Peter Hughes. Vol.8. Oxford: Clarendon Press, 1980.

___. *The Wanderer.* Eds. Margaret Anne Doody, Robert L. Mack and Peter Sabor. Oxford: Oxford University Press, 1991.

Doody, Margaret Anne. *Frances Burney: The Life in the Works.* New Brunswick: Rutgers University Press, 1988.

Du Divorce, Rev. of *The Analytical Review* 7(June 1790):121.

Epstein, Julia. *The Iron Pen: Frances Burney and the Politics of Women's Writing.* Bristol: Bristol Classical Press,1989.

Godwin, William. *Memoirs of the Author of the Rights of Woman.* 1798. Ed. Richard Holmes. Harmondsworth: Penguin, 1987.

Hemans, Felicia. "The Homes of England." *The Poetical Works of Mrs. Felicia Hemans.* Philadelphia: Lippincott, *1855.* 305.

Hibbert, Christopher. *The French Revolution.* Harmondsworth: Penguin, 1982.

Julia. Rev. of. *Critical Review* 69(May *1790):* 592-593.

Mellor, Anne. *Romanticism & Gender.* New York: Routledge, 1993.

Peltier. J. *The Late Picture of Paris.* London: Owen, 1792.

Perry, Sampson. *An Historical Sketch of the French Revolution.* 2 vols. London, 1796.

Price, Richard. *Political Writings.* Ed. D.O. Thomas. Cambridge: Cambridge University Press, 1991.

Richardson, Samuel. *Sir Charles Grandison.* Ed. Jocelyn Harris. 7 vols. Oxford: Oxford University Press, 1986.

Sims, Judy. *Fanny Burney.* Totowa: Barnes & Noble, 1987.

Smith, Charlotte. *The Banished Man.* London: Cadell, 1794.

Sterrenburg, Lee. "Mary Shelley's Monster: Politics and Psyche in *Frankenstein.*" *The Endurance of Frankenstein.* Eds. George Levine and U.C. Knoepflmacher. Berkeley: University of California Press, 1979. 143-171.

Tanner, Tony. *Adultery in the Novel: Contract and Transgression.* Baltimore: Johns Hopkins University Press, 1979.

Ty, Eleanor. "Resisting the Phallic A Return to Maternal Values in *Julia.*" *Unsex'd Revolutionaries.* Toronto: University of Toronto Press, 1993. 73-84.

The Wanderer. Rev. of *Quarterly Review* 11 (April 1814):123-130.

Williams, Helen Maria. *Julia.* 2 vols. London: Cadell, 1790.

___. *Letters from France.* 8 vols in 2. Intro. Janet Todd. Delmar, New York Scholars' Facsimiles & Reprints, *1975.*

___. *Poems on Various Subjects.* London: Whittaker, 1823. Wollstonecraft, Mary. Rev. of *Julia. The Analytical Review* 7(May 1790):97-100.

___. *Mary and The Wrongs of Woman.* Ed. Gary Kelly. Oxford: Oxford University Press, 1980.

Woodward, Lionel. *Helénè-Maria Williams et Ses Amis.* 1930; rpt. Geneva: Slatkine Reprints, 1977.

Having Her Cake and Eating, Too: Ambivalence, Popularity, and the Psychosocial Implications of Ann Radcliffe's Fiction

John Stoler

The literary phenomenon of the late eighteenth century was the Gothic novel, the authorship and readership of which was primarily female. In fact, Tompkins estimates that during the last 30 years of the century, three-fourths of the fiction readers in England were women and that the Gothic novel was their favorite fare (120). The most popular of the many writers cranking out these romances was Ann Radcliffe (1764-1823) who published five Gothic tales between 1789 and 1797. The unprecedented sums of money she was paid for her last two romances attest to her enormous popularity. She received 500 pounds for *The Mysteries of Udolpho* (1794) and 800 pounds—the largest sum ever paid for a novel to that date--for *The Italian* (1797).

The fact of Radcliffe's popularity is beyond dispute, but the reasons for her immense popularity with the general reading public, particularly women, are not nearly so clear because her romances run against the tide of sensibility which dominates late century taste. Sensibility--that combination of delicate feeling, sentimentality, benevolence, and imagination--begins early in the century with the plays of Sir Richard Steele and Nicholas Rowe; finds expression in poetry near mid-century with writers like James Thomson; and works its way into the novel later in the period. A major genre evolving from the School of Sensibility is the Gothic romance, introduced by Horace Walpole in 1764. By this time, the Neoclassical aesthetic based on reason has been mostly replaced by the cult of feeling. Radcliffe's works usually are seen as epitomizing this trend. For example, Sir Walter Scott, an early admirer, called her "the first poetess of Romantic fiction" (214) and in our own century, J.M.S. Tompkins, a seminal critic of Radcliffe, sees her work as a paradigm of Romanticism (248). And, indeed, she does employ distinctively Romantic paraphernalia such as gloomy castles, the Burkean sublime, and supernaturalism as well as fainting and weeping heroines, sensitive heroes, and frightening villains. However, these Romantic elements are only the superficial trappings of Radcliffe's works, which actually are designed to show the dangers of sensibility.

As several scholars have argued--most notably Nelson C. Smith and Robert Kiely--Radcliffe's novels demonstrate that an over-indulgence in sensibility produces irrational behavior by undermining reason. This theme first emerges in *A Sicilian Romance* (1790) in which Julia is described as a typical romance heroine: "An extreme sensibility subjected her to frequent uneasiness; her temper was warm, but generous; she was quickly irritated and quickly appeased; and to a reproof, however gentle, she would often weep, but was never sullen. Her imagination was ardent..." (2:7). Such traits, which were extremely appealing to the female readership of the day, are viewed by Madame de Menon, Julia's governess and a kind of rational norm in the book, as "inimical to [Julia's] future happiness," and so it becomes the governess's "particular care" to mitigate them "in the disposition of her young [pupil]...." Madame de Menon is a suitable person for such a charge, we are told, because of "the powers of her understanding" (1: 8). She urges Julia "to exercise [her] reason" in order to check a too-great reliance on feeling as a guide to conduct and to avoid a vulgar belief in superstition (1: 84).

Perhaps the sternest and most direct warning against the excesses of sensibility is presented early in *Udolpho* when the heroine's father offers the following advice on his deathbed:

> Above all, my dear Emily..., do not indulge in the pride of fine feelings, the romantic error of amiable minds. Those, who really possess sensibility, ought early to be taught that it is a dangerous quality, which is continually extracting the excess of misery, or delight, from every surrounding circumstance. And since, in our passage through this world, painful circumstances occur more frequently than pleasing ones, and since our sense of evil is, I fear, more acute than our sense of good, we become the victims of our feelings, unless we can in some degree command them.... (79-80)

The means of command, Emily's father makes clear, is reason. The book from this point on becomes an object lesson on the dangers of the cult of sensibility, elaborating throughout on the evils of excessive feeling and imagination. Emily herself becomes aware that many of the terrors she experiences come from her frequent deviations from the paths of reason, the consequence of her sensibility, which she calls "a quality, perhaps, more to be feared than desired" (281). The attack on sensibility continues in *The Italian* from a different perspective: here it is the *hero's* ardent imagination and propensity for fine feelings that lead him and the heroine into difficulties that reasonable people could have avoided. Schedoni, the villain, even says that his knowledge of Vivaldi's excessive sensibility enables him to manipulate the young hero.

This strong and consistent opposition to sensibility as a positive trait raises an important question about the high regard in which Radcliffe was held by her contemporaries: How is it that she attains such enormous popularity with the very audience whose literary taste and codes of conduct are based on feeling?

The first response to this question might be that her audience, like Scott, did not perceive her bias against sensibility, taking her work at face value because of her use of conventional romantic devices. It is likely that her contemporary female readership in particular, not classically educated to appreciate Neoclassical values based on reason, dominant earlier in the century and sustained in Radcliffe's period by Dr. Johnson, would eagerly embrace literature which they perceived to be based on feeling rather than reason. According to Samuel Holt Monk, only one of the leading female intellectuals on the London scene at mid-century was proficient in Latin and none knew Greek (216). Even if Monk exaggerates, it is clear that literature based on the Neoclassical aesthetic would have little appeal for the vast majority of female readers. However, these same women could share in the age's common denominator--feeling, which requires no special knowledge or education--and therefore could embrace the cult of sensibility. Not reading as critics and scholars, they took the trappings of Radcliffe's works as their substance. Moreover, female readers turned to fiction not analytically to examine subtexts and themes but as a release. As John Richetti puts it, "Given. . .the severe legal and social limitations upon female action, it is not surprising that novel reading, with its great possibilities for vicarious experience and liberating fantasy, formed an important part of their lives" (126). The Gothic romance in particular provided "opportunity for projected fears and wishes, for fantasies that bear indirectly yet powerfully upon the emotions of women" (Roberts 35). The very ambivalence of Radcliffe's works--the tension between ostensible romantic attitudes and their ironic undercutting by the author's advocacy of standards of reason--may well have had a symbolic appeal. Ann Ronald makes a perceptive observation when she points out that the female readers of Gothic tales often

> get mixed messages--marriage is good/marriage is bad, virile men are fascinating/virile men need castrating, love conquers all/magic conquers all...I believe that the inherent ambiguity is exactly what readers of terror-Gothic tales find so appealing. Unable themselves to define their feelings about marriage, sex, and success, they [are drawn] to the ambivalence they find in their favorite fiction. Indeed, that may well be why it is their favorite fiction. (184)

Radcliffe's novels present mixed messages of their own: they entice their female readers by offering fanciful adventure and by appealing to the vogue of sensibility while at the same time praising the commonsensical values of domesticity to which women were expected to conform in a male-dominated society. Such an ambiguous message reinforces societal codes of behavior while simultaneously allowing a literary escape from them.

The chills and thrills of Radcliffe's novels would have held a special appeal for female readers because the heroine not the hero is central to the action. As Ellen Moers puts it, "In Mrs. Radcliffe's hands, the Gothic novel became a feminine substitute for the picaresque, where heroines could enjoy all the adventures and alarms that masculine heroes had long experienced, far from home, in fiction"(192). Although they are victims, "Mrs. Radcliffe's heroines are not always the simpering puppets which critical tradition has held them to be" (Kiely 70). A heroine like Emily in *Udolpho* usually must engineer her own escapes from danger since she is physically separated from her friends, family, and lover for most of the novel. For example, Emily shows "the strength and reassertion of her will" (Sherman 75) when she attempts to frustrate the machinations of the evil Montoni-- who has incarcerated her in the Castle of Udolpho--by entering into a secret arrangement to get help from Ludovico, a servant. Such scheming and plotting are a far cry from the picaresque deeds of derring-do by male protagonists in earlier literature, but surely women--perceived in Radcliffe's day as helpless, second-class people, powerless and subservient in a male world--would have admired Emily's assertive, independent attempt to take her destiny into her own hands. And they probably cheered her resolve when Montoni attempts to force her to sign her estates over to him and she "positively refused to sign any paper whatever" (379). Later she tells Montoni, "You may find, perhaps, Signor...that the strength of my mind is equal to the justice of my cause; and that I can endure with fortitude, when it is in resistance of oppression." Montoni responds, "You speak like a heroine" (381), and she does and she is. The cheers may well have been even louder for Ellena, heroine of *The Italian,* for her physical and mental toughness, both thought to be distinctively masculine characteristics, when, in her flight from and subsequent capture by Schedoni's agents, she rides on horseback day and night over the most rugged terrain and, fearing poison, goes without food for days without suffering any ill-effects. At San Stephano an attempt is made to force her into a religious order, but she defies the Abbess and refuses to take the veil at the risk of her life. Such hardiness and bravery provided a feminine ideal far-removed from the limited lives of eighteenth-century women "oppressed by needlepoint, whalebone stays, psychic frustrations, shame and babies" (Wolf 2). Bette Roberts points out that "the female reader during the last quarter of the eighteenth century would clearly be attracted to a genre that provided imaginative escape or release from the problematic limitations of her sex role" (34).

Not only her sex role, but the role of sex in the lives of the eighteenth-century woman was also problematic. In Radcliffe's society, male sexuality was acknowledged (even encouraged through the tradition of sowing wild oats on the Grand Tour), but the overt expression of female sexuality was not condoned. Society was more open on the subject during the Restoration--notably in the sexual banter conducted by women in staged comedy--but attitudes began to change at the turn of the century and were reflected in the literature of the early eighteenth century. Lucinda in Steele's *Conscious Lovers* (1722) expresses the prevalent view of proper female behavior with the opposite sex:

> My mother says it's indecent for me to let my thoughts to stray about the person of my husband; nay, she says a maid, rigidly virtuous, though she may have been where her lover was a thousand times, should not have made observations enough to know him from another man when she sees him in a third place...Mama says the first time you see your husband should be at that instant he is made so...To love is a passion, 'tis a desire, and we must have no desires. (145-46)

Although such an attitude was not universally accepted--the speaker herself objects to it and is only stating her mother's views--it certainly prevails in a society dominated by puritanical middle-class social and religious values. The espousal of such values is a major reason for the enormous popularity of Richardson's *Pamela* (1740-41). Pamela sets the standard for female sexual behavior in all of the sentimental novels that follow. This code of behavior demands that even in the face of Mr. B's gropings and sexual enticements, Pamela must remain decorous and essentially passive (becoming active only when she has to physically defend herself against his attempts at rape). She cannot admit, even to herself, that she is sexually attracted to him because, as Lucinda says, a proper young woman is to have no desires, at least none that can be divined by anyone but herself.

On the surface, Radcliffe's romances also equate female virtue with decorum and sexual passivity. For example, in *The Romance of the Forest,* Adeline is attracted to Theodore upon their first meeting, but she keeps a decorous distance from him for most of the novel. Her extreme punctilio is shown just after Theodore rescues her from Montalt's estate where she has been taken against her will and threatened with rape:

> As reflection gradually stole upon her mind, anxiety superseded joy. In the tumult of the late moments, she thought only of escape; but the circumstances of her present situation now appeared to her, and she became silent and pensive; she had no friends to whom she could fly, and was going with a young Chevalier, almost a stranger to her, she knew not whither. (453)

Adeline does not really doubt Theodore's integrity, but she worries about what a censorious world will think about her traveling unchaperoned with a young man. Shortly thereafter when she contemplates the danger Theodore may incur for his intervention in Montalt's affairs and wishes to voice her concern, "She checked the sentence that hung upon her lips, for she perceived that she was unwarily betraying the interest he held in her heart" (454). As Lucinda says, it is improper for a virtuous maiden's thoughts to turn to her love interest, let alone for her to articulate them. Emily shows similar delicacy and decorum throughout *Udolpho.* When Valancourt, whom Emily truly loves, proposes a clandestine marriage, she is shocked by his impropriety, and Radcliffe seems surprised that Emily "did not faint" (155) at the odious suggestion. In *The Italian,* Ellena's sense of decorum is so strong that she implies that perhaps the dangers of her captivity are preferable to escape in the company of a man: "It was true that Vivaldi had discovered her prison, but, if it were possible that he could release her, she must consent to quit it with him; a step from which a mind so tremblingly jealous of propriety as hers, recoiled with alarm, though it would deliver her from captivity" (122). The courteous formality displayed by these three heroines meets the high moral standards expected of eighteenth-century women, and Radcliffe's readers could self-righteously pride themselves on identifying with such models of virtue.

Beneath the surface of this excessively decorous behavior, however, lie powerful symbols of sexual release for female readers, symbols that reinforce "a woman's sense of herself as an essentially sexual creature, something that society has often been at pains to deny" (Wolff 209). In other words, Radcliffe's Gothic fictions allow the female reader to identify with the conventional respectability of the heroine while simultaneously indulging in sexual fantasies which society normally would not condone. Moreover, such an indulgence is safe because the emotions aroused are "under control and...[will] never find overt expression save in another similarly 'safe' fictional world" (Wolff 214).

The most overtly sexual aspect of Radcliffe's novels resides in the descriptions and actions of the villains. Except for Schedoni in *The Italian,* Radcliffe's major villains--Mazzini in *Sicilian Romance,* Montalt in *Romance of the Forest,* and Montoni in *Udolpho*--are described as voluptuaries, and they and some of their villainous associates exude a sexual aura. Mazzini indulges his sybaritic nature by imprisoning his wife so that he can satisfy his sexual appetites in a bigamous marriage with an equally voluptuous woman. However, unlike later villains, there is no suggestion of any sexual attraction between him and Julia because he is her father, and sentimental fiction allows but faint hints of incest and that only between relatives more distant than immediate family. Upon his first appearance in *The Romance of the Forest,* Montalt is described as spirited and fiery, but when he first views Adeline he takes on a "softened aspect and insinuating manners" (353). Although she continues to find Theodore attractive, Adeline also begins to admire the Marquis, who "was polite, affable, and attentive; to manners the most easy and elegant was added the last refinement of polished life. His conversation was lively, amusing, sometimes even witty, and discovered great knowledge of the world..." (368). She finds "the Marquis...so insinuating and affable that her reserve insensibly gave way before it and her natural vivacity resumed its long lost empire" (369). Clearly there is a mutual attraction here, but it abates when Montalt begins to pursue her unrelentingly for his sexual gratification, offering riches if she will give herself to him and, when she will not yield, plotting her rape. The most ambivalent relationship in Radcliffe's work is that between Montoni and Emily in *Udolpho.* When he is first introduced, he is called "handsome" and "Emily felt admiration" for him (122). Although she dreads his visits to her apartment, fearing his designs on her, she frequently throws herself in his way, once falling to the ground before him and embracing his knees to beg him to release her from her imprisonment. Later, watching Montoni's men prepare for a some kind of raid, Emily observes of the dissolute Cavigni that "his graceful and commanding figure, which exhibited the majesty of a hero, had never appeared to more advantage." Excited by the military bearing of these men, she proceeds to "hope, she scarcely knew why, that Montoni would accompany the party..." (302). She experiences the same kind of attraction/repulsion for Montoni that Pamela feels for Mr. B. Unlike Mr. B's obsession with Pamela, however, Montoni shows no sexual interest whatsoever in Emily. The implication is that her fears are at least partly wish fulfillment: she seems to desire being desired. Female readers can enjoy the sexual ambiguity of the situation but not feel morally compromised because nothing sexual happens and the titillating action is confined to the world of fiction.

Radcliffe's physical settings add to the sexually charged atmosphere of her novels. Although she is widely recognized as having introduced extensive nature descriptions into fiction and is lauded for her adept handling of architectural settings, such descriptions and settings have only recently been linked to the sexual aspects of her work. Nina da Vinci Nichols observes that "Metaphorically, place intimates that [the heroine's] most sinister enemy is her own awakening sexuality" (188). Radcliffe does not seem to stress the heroine's awakening sexuality as much as she suggests her unconscious desire for sexual experience, a desire that surfaces in *Udolpho* when Emily connives to be in Montoni's presence even though she fears he and his associates might make unwelcome advances. The heroine's ambivalent fear of sex is increased by the erotic surroundings in which she is placed. For instance, the room to which Adeline is taken when she is abducted by Montalt's servants in *The Romance of the Forest* is described in terms of the traditional banquet of the senses:

> The walls were painted in fresco, representing scenes from Ovid, and hung above with silk drawn up in festoons and richly fringed. The

sofas were of a silk to suit the hangings. From the centre of the ceiling, which exhibited a scene from the Armida of Tasso, descended a silver lamp of Etruscan form...Busts of Horace, Ovid, Anacreon, Tibullus, and Petronius adorned the recesses, and stands of flowers placed in Etruscan vases, breathed the most delicious perfume. In the middle of the apartment stood a small table spread with a collation of fruits, ices, and liquors. (*Romance* 438)

Adeline, confined in such sensual surroundings, is so apprehensive that when Montalt enters the room and approaches her, she faints; at length he revives her, "but when she unclosed her eyes and again beheld him, she relapsed into a state of insensibility..." (440). A little later, the Marquis presses "her to partake of a variety of confectioneries, particularly of some liquors, of which he himself drank freely: Adeline accepted only of a peach" (444). Failing to weaken her resistance to his advances by plying her with liquor, Montalt gives up his seduction attempts for the time being and has Adeline taken to her chamber for the night. The room is decorated with hedonistic paintings and "the steps which were placed near the bed to assist in ascending it were supported by cupids..." (447). The erotic atmosphere of this scene, intensified by the presence of the cupids, increases the anxiety of the heroine and titillates the reader by suggesting that sexual activity may be just around the corner.

These overtly erotic surroundings, however, are not nearly as suggestive as the Freudian overtones of Emily's introduction to the Castle of Udolpho. Both Ann Ronald (179) and Leona Sherman (44-45) note the symbolism of Udolpho's gate, which Radcliffe describes as "of gigantic size..., defended by two round towers, crowned by overlapping turrets...The towers were united by a curtain, pierced and embattled..." (227). The phallic symbolism of the towers and the suggestion of forced vaginal penetration with "pierced and embattled" is reinforced when a servant appears "forcing back the huge folds of the portal, to admit his lord." Emily views "the heavy strength and extent of the whole" with "fearful emotion" and "awe" (227). Sherman finds that Emily's anxiety and the symbolism of the scene produce "a sexual allegory": she says, "Montoni's entrance into the castle suggests a large scale image of sexual penetration...[with] Montoni, a penis, entering the vaginal gate to the womb-like castle through the labia, large folds of the portal" (45). Less obvious than this metaphor for the fear of virginal sexual violation is Sherman's provocative interpretation of Emily's fear of the unlockable back door into her bed chamber:

If rape is a fate worse than death, Emily's horror of entrance via the back door of the "double chamber" indicates to me her fear of a fate still worse than rape, anal penetration. Anal intercourse would be particularly feared as "dirty" and contaminating by any proper eighteenth century virgin, I suspect. Accepting as a basic truth, that what we fear we also wish, I infer Emily's unconscious sexual desires from her inordinate fears, protests, and prolongation of suspense. (49-50)

Sherman may be stretching to make a point here, but such an interpretation is a possibility given the rather obvious Freudian elements of the earlier scene when Emily enters the castle. The female reader of the day was unlikely to perceive the sexual symbolism of such scenes on a conscious level (one even doubts that Radcliffe did), but possibly it reached her on another level, making the novel psychologically attractive. The veiled sexual references in Radcliffe's novels, intensified by the villains' actions and the erotic settings, could provide an expression of the sexual longings of her readers while allowing them to identify with the virtuous heroines who quite properly show no overt interest in sex and resist all sexual advances.

Radcliffe's ambivalence in appealing to the taste for sensibility while advocating the command of feeling through reason and her ability to create proper young heroines while intimating that they have active sexual natures, all put into the context of the kind of adventures previously reserved for men, help explain her widespread appeal to a female readership desperate for some release from the restrictions imposed upon them by a male-structured social code.

Works Cited

Kiely, Robert. *The Romantic Novel in England.* Cambridge: Harvard
    University Press, 1972.

Moers, Ellen. *Literary Women.* New York: Anchor/Doubleday, 1977.

Monk, Samuel Holt. *The Sublime.* New York: MLA, 1935; rpt. Ann
    Arbor: University of Michigan Press, 1960.

Nichols, Nina da Vinci. "Place and Eros in Radcliffe, Lewis, and Bronte."
    The Female Gothic. Ed. Juliann E. Fleenor. Montreal: Eden
    Press, 1983. 187-206.

Radcliffe, Ann. *The Italian, or, The Confessional of the Black Penitents.*
    London: Oxford University Press, 1968.

___. *The Mysteries of Udolpho.* London: Oxford University Press, 1966.

___. *The Romance of the Forest.* In *Three Eighteenth Century Romances.* Ed.
    Harrison Steeves. New York: Scribner's, 1931.

___. *A Sicilian Romance.* 2 vols. London: Hookham, n.d.; rpt. New York:
    Johnson, 1971.

Richetti, John J. *Popular Fiction before Richardson: Narrative Patterns 1700-1739.* Oxford: Clarendon Press, 1969.

Roberts, Bette B. *The Gothic Romance: Its Appeal to Women Writers and Readers in Late Eighteenth-Century England.* New York: Arno, 1980.

Ronald, Ann. "Terror-Gothic: Nightmare and Dream in Ann Radcliffe and Charlotte Bronte." *The Female Gothic.* Ed. Juliana E. Fleenor. Montreal: Eden Press, 1983. 176-86.

Scott, Sir Walter. *Lives of the Novelists.* New York: Dutton, 1910.

Sherman, Leona F. *Ann Radcliffe and the Gothic Romance. A Psychoanalytic Approach.* New York: Arno, 1980.

Smith, Nelson C. *The Art of Gothic: Ann Radcliffe's Major Novels.* New York: Arno, 1980.

Steele, Sir Richard. *The Conscious Lovers.* In *Eighteenth-Century Plays.* Ed. Ricardo Quintana. New York: Random House, 1952. 109-77.

Thornburg, Mary K. Patterson. *The Monster in the Mirror: Gender and the Sentimental Gothic Myth in "Frankenstein."* Ann Arbor: UM Research Press, 1987.

Tompkins, J. M. S. *The Popular Novel in England, 1770-1800.* Lincoln: University of Nebraska Press, 1961.

Wolf, Leonard. "Gothic Novels." *New York Times Book Review* 14 January 1973: 2, 28.

Wolff, Cynthia Griffin. "The Radcliffean Gothic Model: A Form for Feminine Sexuality." *The Female Gothic.* Ed. Juliann E. Fleenor. Montreal: Eden Press, 1983. 207-23.

The Preceptor as Fiend:
Radcliffe's Psychology of the Gothic

David S. Miall

From the perspective of the 1990s, we might regard the Britain of the 1790s as marked by a pervasive neurosis of the social order. Nowhere is this more evident than in the position assigned to women, who were subjected to a range of legal and social disabilities. Although these disabilities were not new to the 1790s, they acquired a special intensity in the aftermath of the French Revolution and the reaction against all things Jacobin. One notable turning point was the eruption of hysteria following the publication of the first edition of William Godwin's *Memoirs* of Mary Wollstonecraft in 1797, which helped ensure that Wollstonecraft's *Vindication of the Rights of Women* (1792) would quickly lose the regard it had initially enjoyed and would soon fall into obscurity. Another instance is the publication of the Gothic novels of Ann Radcliffe, from *The Castles of Athlin and Dunbayne* (1789) to *The Italian* (1797). The extraordinary popular success that the novels enjoyed, together with the rash of third-rate imitations that immediately ensued, suggests that the novels fulfilled an urgent social need.

Despite different aims, the writings of both Wollstonecraft and Radcliffe share one obvious preoccupation, concern with the education of women. Both react, although differently, to the contemporary emphasis in fashionable education on feminine accomplishments and the cult of sensibility. The teacher's role in Radcliffe's novels, however, surpasses that of parent or tutor. Suspense or terror, supernatural intimations, the use of the sublime, and the persecution by powerful men also support pedagogical issues; in this respect the novels point to another principle underlying the neurosis of the 1790s. There was enforced upon most women by the prevailing culture-- that "perpetual babyism" of which Mary Hays complained (97). To be more precise, the Radcliffean Gothic is constructed from a psychological machinery that enacts the predicament of the abandoned child, for whom the only resolution available is the temporary one of wish fulfillment. The novels' significance, and their attraction for their first readers, perhaps lies in that they capture the borderline status of women, neither child nor adult, and portray, albeit in disguised and symbolic form, the attendant disabilities to which their middle-class female readers were themselves victim.

Radcliffe probably did not consciously design her novels to explore such issues; on the contrary, their paradoxes of plot and character suggest conflicted, unconscious materials. No record indicates that Radcliffe received any formal education, although her novels show familiarity with English literature of the eighteenth century, Shakespeare and Milton, and a wide range of travel literature.

Radcliffe as a girl is likely to have been exposed to educational issues discussed within the Wedgwood circle, which also conducted experiments in education involving children of both sexes. The later publication of her novels coincided with an intensification of the debate on female education, which peaked in the 1790s.[1] Her novels make apparent that Radcliffe studied some of the central issues with increasing seriousness and depth of understanding, particularly the place of sensibility and the moral education of women. But the failures of the educational model that Radcliffe came to know, above all its failure to ensure the maturity of women and meaningful social roles, are reflected in the Gothic form intrinsic to Radcliffe's fiction. Thus I interpret the novels as studies in the psychopathology of childhood. Although Radcliffe hoped for an education for women that would secure their virtue and sensitivity, her novels actually hold up to society a distorting mirror in which the preceptors of women appear fiendish and predatory.

That Radcliffe was concerned with education is apparent in all her novels from the first, *The Castles Athlin and Dunbayne,* the opening pages of which consider the heroine's education. Radcliffe's reading of Rousseau's *Emile* is manifest in *The Romance of the Forest,* in which the character of La Luc is modeled on Rousseau's Savoyard vicar. The most elaborate treatment of female education appears in the early chapters of *Udolpho,* where Radcliffe dwells at some length on St. Aubert's upbringing of Emily and his valedictory precepts to her before his death. Radcliffe's views on education cannot be identified with those of St. Aubert, however, but they do correspond significantly with contemporary discussions by such writers as Thomas Gisborne and Hannah More. Her handling of the issues, however, suggests a profound, if unconscious, distrust of the ideological implications of current practices in female education, which she is likely to have encountered with the Wedgwood circle and perhaps even in her own experience.

Radcliffe was related maternally to a wide and influential world. Her uncle was Thomas Bentley, who became the partner of Josiah Wedgwood the potter in 1769, and appears to have been keenly interested in education. Wedgwood's first surviving letter to Bentley, in 1762, refers to "an excellent piece upon *female education,* which I once had the pleasure of reading in MS." and which Bentley is urged to publish (i:2). As a child, she stayed with Bentley at his Chelsea house: the longest period appears to have been autumn, 1771, to spring, 1772, when Ann was aged seven.

Apart from Bentley's direct influence, Ann would also have become aware of contemporary educational practice in the example of Wedgwood's daughter (Susannah [1765-1817]), who was one year younger than Ann and who, upon marrying Dr. Robert Darwin in 1796, became the mother of Charles Darwin. Susannah stayed either with Bentley or at a nearby school in Chelsea called Blacklands between October, 1775, and April, 1778. She seems to have received the standard education for a girl. Wedgwood speaks in one letter of her improvements "as well in her general carriage, & behavior, as in her Music, Drawing &c." (ii:302-03).

Female education when Radcliffe was growing up placed its primary focus on accomplishments. Many critics noted that these were merely utilitarian and subverted any genuine educational achievement. In a diary entry of 1784, for example, Mrs. Thrale (later Piozzi) writes that the female student's "Mother only loads her with Allurements, as a Rustic lays Bird Lime on Twigs, to decoy & catch the unwary Traveller"--that is, a husband (*i:*590-91). Yet these same accomplishments constitute almost all that we first see of an Emily or an Ellena, to whom Valancourt or Vivaldi respond in textbook manner by falling immediately and irrevocably in love. Radcliffe's heroines, in fact, keep themselves occupied very much as contemporary guides recommended. Gisborne's *Enquiry* (1797) suggests improving reading (citing poets that Radcliffe particularly prized, such as Milton, Thomson, Gray, Mason, and Cowper), including poems that instill a sense of the sublime in nature; and he urges the performance of regular acts of charity to poor neighbors (223). Ellena, in *The Italian,* supports herself by selling fine work anonymously through the local convent, somewhat after the manner of Mrs. Cooper's shop in London, noticed by Priscilla Wakefield, which discreetly sold goods made by ladies in deprived circumstances (115).

But in themselves accomplishments are insufficient, as Radcliffe's novels imply. Numerous parents in the 1790s enabled their sons and daughters to ape the manners of the upper classes by attending boarding schools, but as Catherine Macaulay warned, such a polite exterior "is liable to change into a determined rudeness whenever motives of caprice or vanity intervene" (172)--a change that occurs only too readily in the case of a Madame Cheron. The touchstone of Emily's virtue, as with Valancourt, is unswerving sensibility, whether to poetry or to nature. Radcliffe thus accepts the prototype, which so many boarding schools were designed to reproduce, in endowing her heroines with all the fashionable accomplishments; but she shows its limitations at the same time, a stance that ennobles her heroines but weakens their credibility as protagonists.

The physical ideal of womanhood that evolved toward the end of the eighteenth century was equally damaging. Increasing restrictions on body shape and clothing meant, in Lawrence Stone's account, "extreme slimness, a pale complexion and slow languid movements, all of which were deliberately inculcated in the most expensive boarding schools" (*Family* 445). Weakness of body and mind seems to have given women greater sexual attractiveness by increasing the scope for male control. As Fanny Burney's Mr. Lovel in *Evelina* says, "I have an insuperable aversion to strength, either of body or mind, in a female" (361). Radcliffe's heroines, who are capable of little physical exertion and often faint, seem close to this anorexic paradigm. The achievement of this ideal formed the "hidden curriculum" of their schooling. Female education in Radcliffe's period was not primarily about singing or embroidery, it was the enforcement of an anemic, passive, and compliant disposition to prolong women's childhood state constantly on the edge of adolescence. Thus, in *Athlin and Dunbayne,* Mary's indisposition makes her more attractive to Alleyn since it gives her "an interesting languor, more enchanting than the vivacity of blooming health" (110). In her later novels Radcliffe achieves similar effects through the emotional suffering of her heroines, which renders the countenance "more interesting" (*Udolpho* 161).

Besides the heroines' illnesses, their childlike qualities contribute directly to their attractiveness. This is stated most blatantly in *Romance of the Forest* when Theodore reflects that Adeline's charms are best described by the lines of a poem: "Oh! have you seen, bath'd in the morning dew,/The budding rose its infant bloom display;/ When first its virgin tints unfold to view" (*Forest* 172). Wollstonecraft bitterly complains about this view, speaking of women "hanging their heads surcharged with the dew of sensibility" (149). Adeline is also said to be amiable, beautiful, and possessing a simplicity of manners (29); she has a love of virtue that makes it difficult for her to dissemble (160). She has just those virtues, in fact, that More advocates in her *Strictures* (1799) while complaining about women's passion for dress and ornament: "Modesty, simplicity, humility, economy, prudence, liberality, charity are almost inseparably, and not very remotely, connected with an habitual victory over personal vanity and a turn to personal expense" (i:336). Such a heroine is simultaneously strong and weak; she has the finest, best-honed moral sense yet is liable to faint at every critical moment (although the frequency of fainting fits steadily diminishes across Radcliffe's novels).[2] The source of this paradox emerges with the role of moral instruction in Radcliffe's fiction, that is, the use of the precept.

In *Udolpho* the most important education received by the heroine is largely in the form of precepts; yet Radcliffe manages this ambiguously. Emily's father appears to subscribe to a model of female education similar to More's, although his precepts may not be intended at face value. Valancourt's elder brother is described "haranguing on the virtues of mildness and moderation:" (117), which seems to caricature St. Aubert's advice to Emily. Madame Cheron frequently talks in precepts: "she failed not to inculcate the duties of humility and gratitude" (121). More disturbingly, however, Montoni also speaks in maxims, referring to "friends who assisted in rescuing you from the romantic illusions of sentiment...they are only the snares of childhood, and should be vanquished the moment you escape from the nursery" (196)--an even more brutal version of St. Aubert's advice to Emily. Also, Cheron's precepts, based as she claims on "a little plain sense" (204) or "only common sense" (205)*,* are shown actually to involve an acceptance of and complicity in the world of Montoni. Thus, common sense is invoked to disguise patriarchal tyranny. Not coincidently, then, while Montoni attempts to gain control over Emily's property, he talks to her in precepts: "you should learn and practise the virtues, which are indispensable to a woman--sincerity, uniformity of conduct and obedience" (270).[3] Compliance and self-control are demanded by the preceptor in contrast to the method of the teacher, who emphasizes development in the pupil's own interests--a role rarely found in Radcliffe's fiction (except perhaps Madame de Menon in *A Sicilian Romance*).

Therefore, precepts may be the primary agents of the patriarchal perspective, like Polonius's toward his children; preceptors invariably stand against sensibility. Feeling must be controlled by the patriarchal force of reason since feeling is an agent of discovery and would enable its possessor to challenge the preceptor's authority. Thus although Radcliffe seems on the one hand to applaud the precepts of a St. Aubert, on the other hand the tenor of her novels points not only to the inadequacy of such precepts, but also suggests that those who wield them are agents of repression or terror. In educating Emily, St. Aubert strives "to teach her to reject the first impulse of her feelings, and to look, with cool examination, upon the disappointments he sometimes threw in her way" (*Udolpho* 5). But as Robert Kiely notes, "the incongruity between human behavior and moral principles which increases as the book progresses is strangely prefigured in Emily's philosophical father" (71), who fails to abide by his own precepts. While he speaks to Emily of controlling her feelings by reason or mind on the day of her mother's funeral (20-21)—surely a highly premature injunction--he himself is unable in 20 years to overcome his grief at the death of his sister, the poisoned Marchioness de Villerois (660). This prevents his letting Emily know that he even had such a sister, and his silence borders on the culpable, since her knowledge of this piece of family history might have alerted her to the danger of Montoni's guardianship. Whether Radcliffe expected readers to infer that is not clear; her plot lacks internal consistency. The surface structure of her fiction, with its notorious explanations of the supernatural, supports the principles of reason and a rational control over sensibility, and St. Aubert is rendered a mouthpiece for precepts from contemporary treatises on female education. Yet these same principles are repeatedly subverted by Radcliffe's focus on extreme states of feeling. By placing her heroines at the borders of perception and rationality, she enables their aroused sensibilities to acquire knowledge essential for survival.

Radcliffe's handling of sensibility is thus equivocal at a critical juncture of cultural change. More, for example, in her early poem to Mrs. Boscawan "Sensibility," written in 1782, gives her subject high praise: "Unprompted moral! sudden sense of right!" (i:34). In the *Strictures* of 1799, however, several pages warn of the dangers of sensibility, and she withdraws her earlier trust in its moral powers. Women of sensibility, she declares, "are apt to employ the wrong instrument to accomplish the right end. They employ the passions to do the work of the judgment" (i:380). Richard Edgeworth, who brought up his first son on principles of freedom and sensibility inspired by

Rousseau, later moved away from sensibility. When considering female education with his coauthor Maria Edgeworth he advises, "we must cultivate the reasoning powers at the same time that we repress the enthusiasm of *fine feeling*" (i:380). Radcliffe occupies both sides of this debate. She accepts the high valuation placed on women's moral judgment in shaping society through the men they influence (a role on which More and others insisted). For example, Adeline, Emily, and Ellena decide to reject immediate marriage with their suitors at a critical moment, thus becoming moral guides to the men. At the same time, Radcliffe values the impulses of sensibility in ways that More and Edgeworth reprobated. Anticipating the Edgeworths, she makes St. Aubert warn Emily, in terms very similar to ones used by More or the others, "do not indulge in the pride of fine feelings, the romantic error of amiable minds" (*Udolpho* 80). Yet such rational caution has serious limitations.

Contemporary education manuals emphasize keeping females occupied, hence the ceaseless cultivation of accomplishments such as embroidery, etching, drawing, or ribbon work. A woman should carefully avoid reverie, as More stresses. "she, who early imposes on herself a habit of strict attention to whatever she is engaged in, begins to wage early war with wandering thoughts, useless reveries, and that disqualifying train of busy, but unprofitable imaginations. . ." (i:336). But Radcliffe likely would have disagreed with these prescriptions. Although Emily, for instance, feels some guilt when she notices that she has dropped her needlework and fallen into a reverie or has lingered in communion with the falling dusk and the sounds of nature, this is when her sensibilities, thus activated, register the signals that contribute in the long run to her safety. For Emily--and Ellena after her--reverie provides a training in anticipatory reflection on her plight; it becomes soon enough a more urgent interpreting of various critical events and the intellectual study of the logic of different possibilities. To imagine a particular outcome is to gain some control over its actuality. Radcliffe heroines spend an increasing amount of time doing this, as the ratio of action to cogitation decreases over the course of her novels. Reverie strengthens, not weakens, the preparedness of the Radcliffe heroine.

Thus to debate the priority of reason or sensibility in Radcliffe is perhaps fallacious. The novels demonstrate the convergence of these faculties, that sensibility itself is a form of reason. "Despite its elaborate assertions of the need to dominate feeling by reason," as Spacks observes, *"The Mysteries of Udolpho* dramatizes the power of feeling to guide people accurately" (174). Hence, Radcliffe presents an insight that Coleridge or Wordsworth shortly offers more explicitly: for example, Coleridge claims in 1803 that his philosophy is "to make the Reason spread Light over our Feelings, to make our Feelings diffuse vital Warmth thro' our Reason" (*Notebooks* i:1623). Thus feelings, far from coming under the control of reason, increasingly guide the heroine's behavior. Conger, noting this, points to Ellena's sudden suspicion of Spalatro's food in *The Italian* (216): "Here is one of Radcliffe's most successful fictional demonstrations of the finely tuned sensibility in action, and one that presents that sensibility unequivocally as an instinctive survival skill" (*135*). Radcliffe also extends the heroine's clairvoyance to premonitory dreams, such as Adeline's, which lead her to her murdered father's manuscript (*Forest* 108-110), a device in which Radcliffe improves upon a predecessor's strategy (Clara Reeve's *Old English Baron* [1778]).

Despite these significant accomplishments, however, the Radcliffe heroine oddly fails to mature either socially or psychologically. Although she survives her ordeals in order to marry and, presumably, bear children, she seems quite untouched by the succession of terrifying experiences she has had to endure. *Udolpho,* in the words of Macdonald (1989), is "a novel of education in which her heroine starts out with nothing to learn, a novel of maturation in which her heroine ends up as innocent, and as infantile, as she began"(203; also Kiely 78, Howells 9). This analysis applies to the heroines of all the novels. Radcliffe's vision, then, cannot encompass maturation.

At the same time, the Gothic heroine is a survivor, as Punter has suggested (11). Representative of some aspect of actual female experience, she survives amidst the social disruptions and gender politics of the late eighteenth century, but only at the cost of considerable psychological injury. She is the plaything of a Gothic machinery that involves removal of parents, extreme social isolation, prolonged incarcerations, and states of excessive terror, all of which symbolize a predicament that in reality is too threatening to be adequately comprehended.

The repetitive nature of Radcliffe's plots, not only within each novel but from one novel to the next, points to a version of the repetition compulsion which, as Freud pointed out, lies at the root of the uncanny (xvii:238). Endlessly replicating situations of terror, the novels point to a primary source in the experience of women of Radcliffe's generation, the repeated failure to master a trauma. The remarkable success of the Gothic genre she created shows that the representation of woman's predicament in her novels met an urgent cultural need, not just in the 1790s, but in the several decades and numerous imitators that followed.

Although critics have noted that Radcliffe's Gothic fictions occupy a borderland poised between natural and supernatural, the suspense this causes mainly serves plot machinery. Their evocation of a more important psychological borderland generates their genuine emotional power, that between childhood and adulthood. Punter's point that readers of Gothic fiction are free to indulge in regressive visions does not fully account for the experience of women writers such as Radcliffe and their first female readers.[4] Our regressive vision was their historic reality. In this sense, the infantilism imposed on women during the Romantic period perpetuates the psychodrama of early childhood, manifest in the plot of such a novel as *The Italian* as uncanny appearances and connections, meaningful coincidences (portrayed as providence), and the omnipotence of the prevailing powers of church and class. The reader's emotions, in short, reproduce the response to the oppressors that controlled women's lives.

Above all, the hallucinatory symptoms that occur in terror reflect as in a distorting mirror the ethical framework of 1790s patriarchy, with its extravagant and psychotic ethical demands on women. In this world, even the suspicion of a single ethical slip by a woman precipitates a fall into the abyss of ruin; a scale of retribution both disproportionate to the degree of guilt incurred and radically different from that under which men operated.[5] This primitive and savage ethical order imposed upon women suggests one source for the atavism of the Gothic novel, the fear of pollution springing from women's sexuality. As Paul Ricoeur comments on the fear of defilement: "When [man] first wished to express the order in the world, he began by expressing it in the language of retribution" (30). Working out this problematic, Gothic fiction partly desexualizes its heroine by pushing her back across the borders of adolescence, at the same time visiting upon her massive and not entirely explicable sufferings. These serve to increase her sensibilities, sometimes to hallucinatory intensity, but this supplies the heroine's strength as well as her liability. As Emily reflects, "when the mind has once begun to yield to the weakness of superstition, trifles impress it with the force of conviction" (*Udolpho* 634-35). Yet much of the behavior that preserves her at Udolpho derives from just such conviction based upon apparent trifles—a few words, gestures, remote sounds.

But the heroine's hallucinatory perceptions are not merely fantasy, even though they are often factually mistaken at the banal level of plot.

A hallucination intimates repressed unconscious thoughts. As Freud remarks in speaking of "conversion hysteria," a hallucination reproduces in disguised form the actual experience when the repression occurred (xx:111). In this way Radcliffe disguises experiences that properly belong to childhood animism, in which no events are unexplained or random; every strange sight or sound holds a meaning with felt personal significance, even though this significance may be obscure or inexplicable. Just so does a Radcliffe heroine respond with hallucinatory intensity to the sights and sounds around her. Although the animism is later withdrawn in the bathos of explanation (Macdonald 199), the intimated meaning often remains in force and fails to dispel the atmosphere of threat or providence surrounding the heroine. For example, the improbable coincidences on which a Radcliffe plot depends are never adequately explained.[6] Such animism belongs normally only to childhood, but it is likely to be reawakened later in life during crises, such as separation or bereavement. Radcliffe seems to replay such a crisis in the plot of each of her novels, given that her heroines find themselves bereft of one or, usually, both parents, leaving the heroine exposed to vengeful or providential powers beyond her understanding or control. The plot, in other words, replays the regression to animism, in which nothing is meaningless. As Freud says, animism is the "most consistent and exhaustive" and "truly complete" explanation of the universe (xiii:77).

Another dimension of such animism is that the internalizing of the preceptor's voice, which psychoanalytically produces the superego or conscience, is incomplete. Thus the threatening behavior of a Montalt, a Montoni, or a Schedoni echoes the paternal language of the late eighteenth century toward Radcliffe's generation. These men are indeed the "monstrous and phantastic" parental images of which Melanie Klein speaks (250), but in Radcliffe they are not merely outgrowths of the inner aggressive impulses to which Klein attributes them; they correspond to the actual forces that shaped the lives of women and sought to confine them to a state of perpetual adolescence. The Gothic thus embodies the chronic paranoia imposed upon women, easy to ridicule or disregard, as the high culture of the period did only too readily, but representing a genuine persecution nonetheless.

Radcliffe's novels thereby reproduce the kind of persecution often seen in modern clinical reports of hallucinations, especially those of children (Cain 205, Pilowsky 10). At the same time, her heroine's stories invariably replicate the precipitants for hallucinations--being orphaned, isolated, and set adrift in conditions of sensory deprivation (imprisoned in a castle or a convent); in addition, the novels follow a wish-fulfillment pattern, repeated across all the novels, of ultimate rescue by a hero of similar adolescent attributes, following successive failures at deliverance. As the problems faced by women outside the novel are insoluble, neither is development possible for the fictional heroines; they have virtually nothing to learn that would be of use, and they contribute nothing to the society to which they supposedly return after their persecutions cease (and it should be noted that the social structures that facilitated their persecutions remain intact, whether class, religion, or gender). Protagonists such as Ellena and Vivaldi are thus given only the most elementary and contingent of concerns, arising from their love and the various predicaments that follow from it. This is in striking contrast to a Montoni or Schedoni, whose concerns relate to a complex social system of rewards, privileges, and duties. While their concerns are ended only by their deaths, the concerns of Ellena and Vivaldi, by contrast, end with marriage. Hence, the aptness of the refrain that sounds through the last chapter of *The Italian, "O! giorno felice!"* signifying the story's end. With their elementary problems resolved, Ellena and Vivaldi's story has nothing to sustain it beyond a single day. This final freeze frame betrays the stasis in which the women Radcliffe portrays are trapped. Another century must elapse before such Gothic congealment would begin to loosen its regressive grip.

Works Cited

Burney, Fanny. *Evelina*. Ed. Edward A. Bloom. Oxford: Oxford University Press, 1982.

Cain, Albert C. "The Impact of Parental Suicide on Children." *The Child and Death*. Ed. Olle Jane Z. Sahler. St. Louis: Mosby, 1978.

Coleridge, Samuel Taylor. *The Notebooks of Samuel Taylor Coleridge*. Ed. Kathleen Coburn. London: Routledge, 1957-.

Conger, Syndy. "Sensibility Restored: Radcliffe's Answer to Lewis's *The Monk." Gothic Fictions: Prohibition/Transgression*. Ed. Kenneth W. Graham. New York: AMS Press, 1989.

Edgeworth, Richard and Maria. *Practical Education*. 1798. London: Hunter, 1815.

Freud, Sigmund. *The Standard Edition of the Complete Works of Sigmund Freud*, Trans. James Strachey. London: Hogarth Press, 1955-74.

Gisborne, Thomas. *Enquiry Into the Duties of the Female Set*. London: Cadell, 1797.

Hay, Mary. *Appeal to the Men of Great Britain in Behalf of Women*. London: Johnson, 1798.

Howells, Coral Ann. *Love, Mystery, and Misery.* London: Athlone Press, 1978.
Kiely, Robert. *The Romantic Novel in England.* Cambridge: Harvard University Press, 1972.
Klein, Melanie. *Love, Guilt and Reparation and Other Works, 1921-1945.* London: Hogarth Press, 1975.
Macdonald, D. L "Bathos and Repetition: The Uncanny in Radcliffe." *Journal of Narrative Technique* 19:2 (1989), 197-204.
Macaulay, Catherine. *Letters on Education: With Observations on Religious and Metaphysical Subjects.* London: Dilly, 1790.
Mellor, Anne. *Romanticism and Gender.* New York: Routledge, 1993.
Miller, Peter J. Appendix B. "The Education of the English Lady, 1770-1820." Diss. University of Alberta, 1969.
More, Hannah. *Strictures on the Modern System of Female Education. The Complete Works of Hannah More.* New York: Harper, 1835.
Piowsky, Daniel. "Problems in Determining the Presence of Hallucinations in Children." *Hallucinations in Children.* Ed. Daniel Pilowsky and William Chambers. Washington: American Psychiatry Press, 1986.
Piozzi, Hester Lynch. *Thraliana: The Diary of Mrs. Hester Lynch Thrale.* Ed. Katherine C. Balderston. Oxford: Oxford University Press, 1951.
Punter, David. "Narrative and Psychology in Gothic Fiction." *Gothic Fictions: Prohibition/Transgression.* Ed. Kenneth W. Graham. New York AMS Press, 1989. 1-27.
Radcliffe, Ann. *The Castles of Athlin and Dunbayne.* 1821; rpt. New York Arno: Press, 1972.
___. *The Italian.* Ed. Frederick Garber. Oxford: Oxford University Press, 1981.
___. *The Mysteries of Udolpho.* Ed. Bonamy Dobrée. Oxford: Oxford University Press, 1980.
___. *The Romance of the Forest.* Ed. Chloe Chard. Oxford: Oxford University Press, 1986.
Ricoeur, Paul. *The Symbolism of Evil.* Trans. Emerson Buchanan. Boston: Beacon Press, 1969.
Spacks, Patricia Meyer. *Desire and Truth: Functions of Plot in Eighteenth-Century English Novels.* Chicago: Chicago University Press, 1990.
Stone, Lawrence. *The Family, Sex and Marriage in England 1500-1800.* New York Harper, 1977.
___. *Road to Divorce: England 1530-1987.* Oxford: Oxford University Press, 1990.
Wakefield, Priscilla. *Reflections on the Present Condition of the Female Sex; with Suggestions for Its Improvement.* London: Johnson, 1798.
Wedgewood, Josiah. *Letters of Josiah Wedgewood:1762-1795.* 3 Vols.

Ed. Katherine Eufemia Farrer. 1903; rpt. Manchester: Morton, 1973.
Wollstonecraft, Mary. A Vindication of the Rights of Women. 2nd ed.
Ed. Carol H. Poston. New York: Norton, 1988.

Endnotes

[1] Miller lists the number of publications devoted to the "character, duties and education of women" in Britain: in the decade beginning 1760 there were 16, in 1770, 23; 1780,25; 1790, 41; 1800, 35; 1810,13 (492-98).

[2] Someone faints on average after every 11 pages in *Athlin* (converting the page sizes of the Arno reprint to those of the Oxford editions), 18 pages in *Sicilian*, 40 pages in *Forest*, 48 pages in *Udolpho*, and 52 pages in *The Italian*.

[3] Anne Mellor's recent discussion of the sublime in *Udolpho* touches on this question: "Radcliffe's point is clear: the deepest terror aroused by the masculine sublime originates in the exercise of patriarchal authority within the home" (93).

[4] Punter refers to our pleasure in "being able to peer backwards through our own personal history, because all psychotic states are simply perpetuations of landscapes which we have all inhabited at some stage in our early infancy" (8).

[5] Even Radcliffe's preoccupation with the incarceration of her heroines seems less a mere fantasy in light of how often wives were forcibly and legally confined by their husbands (Stone, *Road* 164-69).

[6] Perhaps the most absurd examples are from *Forest*, where the fleeing La Mottes and Adeline end up at the Abbey of St. Clair, which just happens to be owned by Adeline's uncle, and when Peter and Adeline flee to his village in the Savoy, Adeline just happens to end up living with La Luc, the father of her lover Theodore, but all the novels depend in some degree on such coincidences.

The Treatment of Women in the Novels of Charlotte Turner Smith

Joseph Rosenblum

When Mariana of the moated grange appears veiled in the final act of *Measure for Measure,* the Duke attempts to identify her by placing her in a category that expresses some relationship to a man: a maid (and so subject to her father), a widow, or a wife. When she rejects all three options, the Duke concludes, "Why, you are nothing then" (V.i.177). This same issue of female definition informs Samuel Richardson's *Clarissa,* which demonstrates the truth of the Duke's observation in that the eponymous heroine's efforts to achieve an independent identity in a male-dominated world lead to her annihilation. Women writers of the seventeenth and eighteenth centuries wrestled with this issue: Mary Astell, Judith Drake, Lady Mary Chudleigh, Lady Mary Wortley Montague, Elizabeth Thomas, Mary Wollstonecraft, and Charlotte Turner Smith. Through her fiction Smith attacked patriarchal laws and attitudes. By rejecting conventional labels (like those that the Duke sought to impose on Mariana) and stereotypical portraits, Smith advocates a new and equal relationship between the sexes.

Smith's concern is evident even in her choice of protagonists. Her first three novels take their names from their female heroines-- Emmeline, Ethelinde, and Celestina. *Desmond* (1792), named for a man, in fact concentrates on the life of Geraldine Verney; *The Old Manor House* (1794) concerns itself as much with Monimia as with her lover, Orlando. *Montalbert* (1795) tells the story of Rosalie Lessington; *Marchmont* (1796) is the tale of Althea; and *The Young Philosopher* (1798) deals less with the title character, George Delmont, than with

Laura Glenmorris and her daughter, Medora. These women may marry, but, as Mary Anne Schofield writes in "The Witchery of Fiction," they demonstrate that women "do not have to accept the lies men offer, that they have a right to their own minds, selves, and lives" (186).

In *Marchmont* Smith objected to her readers' expectations of the stereotypical heroine: "too much reason and self command destroy the interest we take in her distresses" (1:179). Undeterred by this popular attitude, Smith insisted on portraying women who are rational without being heartless. The first chapter of Smith's first novel rejects the image of the helpless heroine. When Emmeline's friend and protector, Mrs. Carey, dies, Emmeline does not yield "to tears and exclamations" but instead considers "how she should best perform all she now could do for" the deceased (*Emmeline* 6). The book, like all of Smith's others, is filled with crying, and Smith is sentimentalist enough to treat a lack of feeling as worse than a deficiency of reason. Yet her heroines, no less than her heroes, possess both qualities in proper measure.

Emmeline demonstrates more self-control than her lover, Delamere, whose inability to master his passion renders him an unsuitable mate. Godolphin, whom she marries, is more rational than his rival, but Emmeline is at least his equal, and sometimes his superior, in reason. Mrs. Stafford in this novel again belies the image of female irrationality. She helps educate Emmeline, who appreciates--as Mr. Stafford does not--"the charms of her conversation, the purity of her heart, and the softness of her temper, [her] advantages of a polished education, and that ease of manner which the commerce of fashion can supply" (*Emmeline* 43,70). Mrs. Stafford negotiates with her husband's creditors after he has squandered the family's money; Smith thus demonstrates that the wife has more business sense than the husband. Between the lines she is arguing that women should not be excluded from commerce on the grounds of incapacity.

In Geraldine Verney (*Desmond*) Smith presents another woman superior to her husband. He is "the sport of every wild propensity or rather of every prevailing fashion," whereas Geraldine "immediately...sees the ridiculous, and...shrinks from vice and folly" (1:2-3). At the outset of the novel Smith reverses the conventional portrayal of reasonable man and flighty woman, not so much to denigrate males as to demonstrate that neither sex has a monopoly on folly or virtue. Geraldine's brother is also her mental inferior, unable to resolve on any course of action, even of pleasure. In *The Old Manor*

House Monimia demonstrates more presence of mind than her lover, Orlando, when they are surprised during one of their innocent but secret late night meetings. Later, when he learns that he must leave England to join his regiment in America, he is distraught; Monimia must calm his anxiety. Through adversity Althea (*Marchmont*) "acquired that fortitude and strength of mind which gave energy to an understanding naturally of the first class" (1:179). She prefers the tranquility of solitude to the "wretchedness to which a union with Mohun would have condemned her" (2:234). Lucy Marchmont similarly displays "good sense and courage" (3:156) and what Schofield calls a "commonsense attitude toward life" (171).

Though Smith writes romances, she redefines the romantic heroine as one who controls her own life, who inscribes her own text and does not let men write that story for her, as when Rosalie Lessington rejects an arranged marriage and weds Montalbert in secret or when Geraldine Verney literally writes much of the epistolary novel *Desmond*. Laura Glenmorris's elopement (*The Young Philosopher*) echoes Clarissa's flight with Lovelace both in motivation and execution, but the consequences for Smith's heroine are happier, showing that women can seize control of their own lives without catastrophe. Laura Glenmorris expresses the new meaning of romance and romantic when she exclaims,

> If it be romantic to dare to have an opinion of one's own, and not to follow one formal tract, wrong or right, pleasant or irksome, because our grandmothers and aunts have followed it before; if not to be romantic one must go through the world with prudery, carefully settling our blinders at every step, as a cautious coachman hoodwinks his horses heads; if a woman, because she is a woman, must resign all pretensions to being a *reasoning* being, and dares neither look to the right nor to the left, oh! may my Medora still be the child of nature and simplicity, still venture to express all she feels, even at the risk of being called a strange romantic girl. (*The Young Philosopher* 2:14-15)

Smith's rhetoric reenforces her emphasis on female independence: she refers only to female ancestors, and she demotes to animals those women who allow men to control them and shape their views.

George Delmont learns from his mother--not a male tutor--"to reason on every thing..., instead of seeing all objects, as they are represented, through the dazzling and false medium of prejudice, communicated from one generation to another" (1:86-87). His friend Mrs. Glenmorris shows physical as well as mental courage and stamina in effecting her escape from her Highland Scots captors, the Kilbrodies, living for weeks in an unheated stone shelter, and walking many miles without collapsing.

In the preface to *Desmond* Smith speaks in her own voice to refute misogynist aspersions on female intelligence, noting that women "are censured as affecting masculine knowledge if they happen to have any understanding; or despised as insignificant triflers if they have none" (iv). She goes on to observe that

> knowledge which qualities women to speak or to write on any other than the most common and trivial subjects, is supposed to be of so difficult attainment, that it cannot be acquired but by the sacrifice of domestic virtues, or the neglect of domestic duties.—! however may safely say, that it was in the *observance,* not in the *breach* of duty, *I* became an Author,...

a course required because "the affairs of my family [are] most unhappily in the power of men" (iv-v). She also defends her writing about the French Revolution because politics is a suitable subject for women. The novel is filled with references demonstrating Smith's wide reading in various languages, and her repeated use of botanical Latin in *The Young Philosopher*--the epigrams of which once more reveal her command of literature--links her to her well-read heroines. Smith consistently invokes other female writers, including such well-known figures as Wollstonecraft, Susanna Centlivre, and Sarah Fielding, but also more obscure authors like Madame Des-Houliere and an unnamed friend who supplies the ode ascribed to Geraldine Verney in the third volume of *Desmond.*

Smith's advocacy of modern as opposed to classical literature poses another challenge to male intellectual hegemony. Emmeline turns from black-letter books to writers of the English Renaissance and Augustan eras. (In fact, black-letter texts printed in the Renaissance were likely to be aimed at a popular audience, whereas the Roman-letter texts were intended for the classically trained elites.) By the end of the eighteenth century, black letter suggested the medieval, the Latinate, and the male-dominated clerisy. Smith draws on the contemporary impression, not the historical reality here. Like Emmeline, Mrs. Stafford cultivates her mind by reading "the best authors in the modern languages" (*Emmeline*

43). The traditional male preserve of classical education thus appears unnecessary to achieve culture; nor is attending a university, another male bastion, a guarantee of or prerequisite for moral or intellectual excellence. Orlando's older brother attends Oxford for three years but is foolish and mean-spirited, whereas Orlando, who reads in Mrs. Rayland's library, proves a far better person. There may be significance in the fact that this library belongs to a woman; certainly there is significance in the fact that Monimia receives the same education as Orlando. In *The Young Philosopher* Oxford fails to improve Middleton Winslow, whereas George Delmont receives excellent instruction from his mother.

Delmont's respect for Medora's intelligence marks him as one of Smith's heroes. Just as the novels seek to promote female independence and self-assertion, they also attempt to teach male readers how they should treat women and to instruct female readers on what sort of man to choose for husband or friend. Sir Richard Croft's villainous nature manifests itself in his belief "that for a woman to affect literature is the most horrid of all absurdities; and for a woman to know anything of business, is detestable!" (*Emmeline* 236). The wicked lawyer Brownjohn in *The Young Philosopher* has no respect for women's understanding; Geraldine Verney's husband, who tries to sell his wife to the Duke de Romagnecourt, "has the most contemptible opinion" of women's minds and believes that they are good for nothing but to make a show while we are young, and to become nurses when we are old" (*Desmond* 2:32). By way of contrast Bethel respects Geraldine's opinions and discusses the French Revolution with her. Desmond, too, trusts her judgment and lets her decide on her own not to accompany the duke back to France.

As Smith rejects the conventional weak, uneducated, unintelligent heroine, so she redefines the proper relationship between the sexes as one based on equality in all matters. Adelina Trelawny (*Emmeline*), married to a husband unworthy of her, is seduced by George Fitz-Edward and bears his child. At the end of the novel, Adelina's husband having conveniently died, Fitz-Edward offers to marry his former mistress. Adelina declines the match, but Smith endured some sharp criticism for suggesting the possibility of Adelina's happy union with her seducer. The *Analytical Review* for July, 1788, attacked the book's dangerous tendency "to debauch the mind, and throw an insipid kind of uniformity over the moderate and rational prospects of life, consequently *adventures* are sought for and created, when duties are neglected, and content despised" (33). The author of this attack was

Wollstonecraft, but if she was assuming the voice of conventional morality to please her readership, Smith was willing to challenge the accepted notions of hers. Henry James Pye similarly objected in *The Spectre* that Smith made "adultery amiable, and perfidy meritorious, and [dismissed] the perpetrators of both to respectability, to honour, and to happiness" (*Emmeline* x).

Smith may have been unwilling in 1788 to offend public morality so far as to allow Adelina and Fitz-Edward to marry. Perhaps, though, Adelina's refusal of his proposal was meant to demonstrate that female empowerment and liberation would not lead to a flouting of conventional morality. Patriarchal control that forced Adelina to wed leads to an illicit union with Fitz-Edward because of the unhappy marriage. Freed from parental and marital constraints, Adelina chooses separation from Fitz-Edward. *The Young Philosophers* again attacks patriarchal control of female affection. Commenting on Sir Harry Richmond's refusal to allow his daughter to marry the man she loves, Smith writes, "These are indeed among the wrongs of woman" (4:166).

In *Desmond* Smith went farther than she had in 1788 in arguing for sexual equality. Smith's hero loves and eventually marries the wife of another. While he is waiting for Geraldine Verney's husband to die, Desmond carries on an affair with Josephine Montfleuri; the liaison produces a child. Not only does Smith not condemn either party, but Josephine, unlike Adelina, will remarry if, as is likely, her husband has been killed. In *The Old Manor House* Orlando and Monimia repeatedly meet secretly in the library or the heroine's bedroom, and in *The Young Philosopher* Mrs. Glenmorris and her daughter live with George Delmont and Armitage. As Florence Hilbish observed, "Since there is no need for this approach to the verge of impropriety in order to advance the story, it seems clear that the author's purpose is to break down false conventions and to show the innocent and intimate friendship that may exist among individuals whose lives are clean and pure" (324). Deterred by rumors of an illicit relationship with Armitage, Mrs. Glenmorris refuses to ask for his help when she goes to London; as a consequence of these false scruples her daughter is abducted and she herself is confined in a madhouse. Smith thus warns against the false delicacy that substitutes prudery for common sense.

Smith's belief in the equality of the sexes manifests itself in the androgyny of some of her major figures. Her heroines demonstrate physical bravery and mental fortitude traditionally regarded as masculine. Conversely, her heroes are as likely as their female counterparts to burst into tears. Geraldine Verney praises Desmond's "disdain of personal danger" but also his "manly tenderness--such generous sensibility for the feelings of others!" (*Desmond* 2:5). Later Geraldine writes, "There is nothing...in my opinion, so graceful, so enchanting, in a young man, as this tenderness towards children" that Desmond exhibits (2:254). Geraldine herself combines traits of both genders, "the softness of manners of her own sex [with] a strength of understanding which we [men] believe peculiar to ours" (2:97). Orlando physically resembles his grandmother and, like Desmond, displays "manly tenderness" (*The Old Manor House* 426). George Delmont unites courage, intelligence, and "softness of heart" (*The Young Philosopher* 1:98).

At the end of *The Young Philosopher* the Glenmorris women leave England for America. With this work Smith abandoned adult fiction, perhaps because like Laura and Medora Glenmorris she sensed that England was not ready to accept her views on gender roles and sexual equality. As a reformer Smith may be viewed as a failure, but, as her only biographer has remarked, "By delineating the adventures of a heroine instead of a hero and by revealing woman as she is rather than according to man's fancy of the ideal,...she greatly advanced the status of the heroine of the novel" (Hilbish 545). Smith spoke out against the wrongs of women and in the process helped redefine literary response, if not societal attitudes, to these issues. What Schofield observes of eighteenth-century women writers in general is particularly applicable to Smith:

> The unmasking of the romance and its heroine, like the uncovering of the masquerade and the masquerader, reveals the woman as a different person from that presented in the popular ideologies. Looking underneath, one discovers that the heroine is neither helpless and submissive, nor is she enthralled with the capitulation and condescension of the romance story. (190)

Works Cited

Elliott, Pat. "Charlotte Smith's Feminism: A Study of *Emmeline* and *Desmond.*" Ed. Dale Spender. *Living by the Pen: Early British Women Writers.* New York: Teachers College Press, 91-112.

Hilbish, Florence. *Charlotte Smith: Poet and Novelist.* Philadelphia: University of Pennsylvania Press, 1941.

Schofield, Mary Anne. *Masking and Unmasking the Female Mind: Disguising Romances in Feminine Fiction, 1713, 1799.* Newark: University of Delaware Press, 1990.

___. "The Witchery of Fiction: Charlotte Smith: Novelist." Ed. Dale Spender.

   Living by the Pen: Early British Women Writers. New York: Teachers College Press, 1992, 177-187.

Smith, Charlotte. *Desmond: A Novel.* London: Robinson, 1790.

___. *Marchmont: A Novel.* London: Sampson Low, 1796.

___. *The Young Philosopher: A Novel.* London: Cadell and Davies, 1798.

___. *The Old Manor House.* Ed. Anne Henry Ehrenpreis. London: Oxford University Press, 1969.

___. *Emmeline: The Orphan of the Castle.* Ed. Anne Henry Ehrenpreis. London: Oxford University Press, 1971.

Spender, Dale, ed. *Living by the Pen: Early British Women Writers.* New York: Teachers College Press, 1992.

Jane Austen's Opacities

Laura Dabundo

Like Wordsworth and the other great poets of her times, Jane Austen balances her art between silence and speech and knows the limits beyond which speech cannot proceed.[1] One of the principal insights of the Romantic movement in England is this very privileging of silence. The Grecian urn, the ruined cottage, Mont Blanc, and midnight frost are all exemplary of this poetic attempt to capture the ineffable, to point to something that cannot be spoken but yet for which the gesture is the poem, the message, and the meaning. Yet whereas Wordsworth, for instance, deploys many characters in his poetry who are rudely educated, roughly hewn, lower-class partisans for whom speech is indeed difficult and their purchase upon it too inadequate for the dimensions of their experience, Austen's characters are fully comfortable in their idiom. If they do not speak or if their words are less than equal to their emotion or their truth, it is their decision, or, even more significantly, that of their author. In both, the poetry and novel of the early nineteenth century, however, instances occur in which the words are defeated; the blankness, embraced.

I believe that Austen is like the contemporary poets, not perhaps in the form of art she deploys, but certainly in the attitudes and customs with which she animates it. Therefore, one might posit that one of the achievements of early nineteenth-century literature, foreshadowing the deconstructionists perhaps, concerns the spaces and silences between the words, the gaps and pauses that punctuate speech but yet have meaning. (Obviously, much else concerns English Romanticism, but for purposes of this essay my focus on these writers is restricted to what they don't write).

This interest in a fiction writer raises, of course, the broader issue of her sympathetic convergence in general with the leading male poets of the day, whose aesthetic would increasingly come to represent the age. Four particular instances of overlap come to mind, including two that seem to engage specific canonical Romantic poems.

In *Sense and Sensibility* (published 1811, but first written more than a decade before), a tantalizing interlude anticipates and corrects Percy Shelley. Following the over-heated transports of emotional, passionate Marianne, the outwardly practical but inwardly long-suffering Elinor remonstrates: "'It is not every one who has your passion for dead leaves'" (76). Even if the Dashwood sisters are at least one and possibly two decades in advance of Shelley's magisterial tribute to the West Wind (Reiman and Powers 221 n.1), still few would deny, I imagine, that Marianne in time would swoon over Shelley's verse, which would probably prove to be a trifle too vaporous for her elder sister's taste, a reasonably acceptable contiguity that nevertheless reinforces the implication that this poetry and these people inhabited the same time and space. That is to say, the sentiment accords even if the dates do not.

Second, *Persuasion*, the last novel (published posthumously in 1818), also participates in the Romantic milieu by looking forward to another Romantic poetic staple associated with dying leaves. Anne Elliot finds delight in strolling out-of-doors on a lovely fall day, amid "the tawny leaves and withered hedges," meanwhile

> repeating to herself some few of the thousand poetical descriptions extant of autumn, that season of peculiar and inexhaustible influence on the mind of taste and tenderness, that season which has drawn from every poet, worthy of being read, some attempt at description, or some lines of feeling. (82)

This passage harmonizes Anne with the Romantic sensibility that finds Keats's "season of mists and mellow fruitfulness" both "peculiar and inexhaustible," even as it links Austen with Keats, offering in advance a bouquet for the poet's exquisite verse, inspired by his own walk through fields and hedgerows (written in 1818, published in 1819; Perkins 1204).

Third, a somewhat more satisfying connection with the Romantic period's Lake Poets is established for Austen by *Pride and Prejudice* (begun probably in the 1790s but published in 1813) when Elizabeth Bennet expresses her exhilaration, similar to Marianne Dashwood's raptures, at the prospect of her excursion to Lakeland: "'What delight! What felicity! You give me fresh life and vigour. Adieu to

Susan Ferrier's Allusions: Comedy, Morality, and the Presence of Milton

Angela Esterhammer

Virtually all of Susan Ferrier's commentators, including her few modern critics, agree in seeing her work as conflicted, marked by an ongoing struggle between her talent for robust humor and her inclination toward a conservative, pious Christianity. This conflict is intensified by her situation as a female writer whose subject is women's lives and choices. On the one hand, Ferrier's satire is leveled against traditional male authority, and she sympathetically portrays the sentimental education of young women; on the other hand, all her heroines respect the authority of parents or guardians and end up in appropriate, sanctioned marriages. Depending on their own ideological bent, Ferrier's critics tend to see these conflicts as the result of either morality and serious purpose giving way to an uncontrollable urge for comedy or else an embryonic, subversive feminism capitulating to the habits of a religious upbringing. Thus W. M. Parker, writing in the 1960s, quotes a critic of the 1840s who commended Ferrier's eventual "command over the higher passions and more tender emotions as well as over the ludicrous and the grotesque" (qtd. in Parker 17), though Parker still claims that "she had not sufficient control over her exaggerations" (17-18). Conversely and more recently, Nancy Paxton applauds Ferrier's "wonderful joke" on serious readers (28) and the "natural wit" of her heroine (24), aspects that undercut what Paxton appears to characterize as the flaws of Ferrier's first 'novel: "the conventional values of filial obedience, Christian self denial, and the sanctity of marriage" (20).

Rather than treating either lively satire or moral integrity as the reality of Ferrier's art constantly struggling to assert itself in the face of repression, I would like to examine the extent to which these two qualities are focused and combined in her allusions. Despite the haphazard quality of her education, Ferrier's prose is marked by frequent references to and echoes of Shakespeare, Milton, Pope, Johnson, and other canonical authors in English, French, and occasionally Italian. Milton provides an especially interesting case study: as the voice of patriarchal authority in the tradition of Christian epic, he has often been characterized as an overpowering and anxiety-provoking influence on Romantic writers. The masculinist Milton of Harold Bloom's *Anxiety of Influence* has more recently been identified by Sandra Gilbert and Susan Gubar as the great inhibitor of nineteenth-century women writers, while Joseph Wittreich, always more optimistic about Milton's influence whether on William Blake or Mary Wollstonecraft, contends that eighteenth-century and Romantic women were more likely to regard Milton as an advocate of equality and revolution. Gilbert and Gubar propose two alternative responses to Milton "in which almost all writing by women can be subsumed" (220): on the one hand, there is "the option of apparently docile submission to male myths" (219); on the other, "the option of secret study aimed toward the achievement of equality," which leads to "the alternative of rewriting *Paradise Lost* so as to make it a more accurate mirror of female experience" (219-220). Wittreich, however, argues that "there are more than the two [paradigms of female response] delineated by Gilbert and Gubar" (12), and his *Feminist Milton* shores up evidence for another major category of response: the approbation of female readers who realized that, as Wittreich believes, Milton's poetry subtly subverts the very orthodoxies that male readers claim it upholds.

In the context of growing interest in the reception of Milton among women readers and writers, Ferrier's work may be seen as illustrating yet another type of response. On one level, Ferrier seems a model of "docile submission," quoting Milton with apparent acceptance of his moral universe and his canonical authority. Yet she also recognizes how his reputation for elevated discourse can generate irony and humor when his poetry is set against the more mundane concerns of the novel of manners. Using Miltonic allusions to augment the moral resonances of her plots, but also, and sometimes simultaneously, to create comic hyperbole, Ferrier displays an adept use of the Tradition and an attitude toward it that is markedly less anxiety-ridden than that of contemporaries like Wordsworth, Blake, and Keats or, for that matter, Wollstonecraft and Mary Shelley.

The first of Ferrier's three novels, *Marriage* (1818), is rich in direct allusions because each of its 68 chapters is prefaced by at least one epigraph. The great majority of the epigraphs for the early chapters are drawn from the works of Milton, and all of them contribute to Ferrier's satirical portrait of the vapid and spoiled Lady Juliana Douglas. They do this by, in effect, expressing Lady Juliana's point of view (and perhaps it is not unimportant that the Englishman John Milton is made to speak for the English noblewoman Juliana as she enters the Scottish Highlands), but in a way that underscores the distinction between Milton's solemnity and Lady Juliana's frivolity. Having eloped with the dashing Scottish captain Henry Douglas, Lady Juliana follows him to his father's Highland castle, an environment that the spoiled Englishwoman finds unbearably crude, uncivilized, and deadly dull. In apparent sympathy with her, the epigraph to the third chapter quotes the words of Moloch in *Paradise Lost* (II.85-86), as he speaks out in the Satanic council for open war against the Almighty: "What can be worse/Than to dwell here?" (I.15). With these economical lines, Ferrier expresses Lady Juliana's conviction that the Highlands are Hell, her belief that she herself belongs in a higher place and has unjustly been driven from bliss, and her determination to resist or make her own form of war on all who oppose her. Yet at the same time we are struck by two contrasts: an ironic appearance between the beautiful Lady Juliana and the devil Moloch and one of character between the profound courage of Moloch ("the strongest and the fiercest Spirit that fought in Heav'n" *PL* II.44-45) and Juliana's incredible superficiality.

The Douglas castle, Glenfern, is alternately cast as Hell and as Paradise. Lady Juliana clearly regards it the way Satan regards Hell, and her exclamation on first catching sight of Glenfern--"Good God, what a scene! How I pity the unhappy wretches who are doomed to dwell in such a place!" (1:11)--is amplified by a later epigraph that employs Satan's orders to the rebel angels before he leaves on his quest to corrupt humankind: "If there be cure or charm/ To respite or relieve [misquoted for "deceive"], or slack the pain/Of this ill mansion" (1:78; cf. *PL II* .460-62). If these echoes of *Paradise Lost* augment the comedy of Lady Juliana's behavior by exposing the excesses of her response to her situation, it is not insignificant that they also ally her with the devil. In the rest of the novel, Juliana's egotistical behavior is more explicitly and seriously destructive of the peace and happiness of her husband and her daughters Adelaide and Mary.

But the main function of the Miltonic epigraphs in the early chapters of *Marriage* is to satirize Juliana's behavior by expressing her point of view in the elevated language of literary tradition, then juxtaposing that elevation with her pettiness and the bumpkinish behavior of the Douglas clan. In a chapter that describes the after-dinner entertainments at Glenfern, a verse from "L'Allegro" (135-36), "And ever against eating cares,/Lap me in soft Lydian airs" (1:25), expresses Juliana's desire for pleasure and diversion, which is indifferently met by her sister-in-law Bella's thunderous spinet playing. Similarly, a line that describes Eve's preparation of a meal for Raphael and Adam, "What choice to choose for delicacy best" (1:36; cf. *PL* V.333), headlines a chapter that is completely taken up with the Douglases' futile attempts to offer the fastidious (and pregnant) Juliana something that she can stomach for breakfast.

Ferrier's funniest and most significant allusions to *Paradise Lost* concern the Edenic books--the section of the epic that, according to Wittreich, was preferred by many female readers of her time (*56, 63*). Milton's description of Eden, "Nature here! Wanton'd as in her prime, and played at will/Her virgin fancies" (1:64; cf. *PL* V.294-96), ironically prefaces a chapter of *Marriage* that is not about nature at all, but about the chaotic, uncultured behavior characteristic of the Glenfern household, especially when it is trying to make an impression on visitors. The kind-hearted but fussy aunts Jacky, Grizzy, and Nicky apply the wrong medicine to every disorder; the jittery servant Donald spills whipped cream on guests; and Henry Douglas's five tomboyish sisters vainly try to present a feminine appearance by dressing up in "thin muslin gowns, made by a mantuamaker of the neighbourhood in the extreme of a two year-old fashion, when waists were *not*" (1:65) (a phrase that itself echoes Milton's description of Chaos, when "the Sun/ Was not" *PL* VII.247-48).

The chapter that introduces the Douglases' neighbors, Sir Sampson and Lady Maclaughlan, is prefaced by lines from *Paradise Lost* that were frequently cited by Ferrier's contemporaries in support of a variety of ideological positions:

> Though both
> Not equal, as their sex not equal seemed—
> For contemplation he, and valour formed;
> For softness she, and sweet attractive grace.
> (I:55; cf. *PL* IV.295-98)

Sir Sampson and Lady Maclaughlan are two of the novel's most successful comic figures, and the Miltonic epigraph intensifies Ferrier's satire by its complete misrepresentation of their characters. The couple is nothing if not "unequal," but this is because Lady Maclaughlan, far from being soft and graceful, is domineering towards everyone, but especially towards the invalid Sir Sampson, whose withered frame hardly lives up to the strength of his Miltonic name. One might assume that Ferrier's purpose is to critique Milton by depicting a woman who, if somewhat overpowering, is intelligent and independent--that is, that Ferrier agrees with Wollstonecraft when she denounces Milton's insinuation "that we were beings only designed by sweet attractive grace, and docile blind obedience, to gratify the sense of man when he can no longer soar on the wing of contemplation" (Wollstonecraft 88). Yet Ferrier's point of view is at once more conservative and more complex than this. In portraying a couple in which the authority lies almost entirely with the wife, Ferrier does not undo Milton's hierarchy, but only reverses it for comic purposes; indeed, she characterizes Lady Maclaughlan, with her "masculine habiliments" (1:64) and her walking stick, as unattractively male. Moreover, the same chapter that introduces the un-Miltonic Sir Sampson and Lady Maclaughlan to us introduces Henry Douglas and Lady Juliana to them, and the younger couple does appear to personify Milton's description of a noble Adam and a sweet, feminine Eve. Thus far in *Marriage,* Ferrier uses Miltonic allusions deftly and economically to complicate perspective and thereby heighten the comedy of behavior and situations, but she does not attempt direct attacks on Milton's moral universe.

The infamous concluding line of the above passage--"Hee for God only, shee for God in him" (*PL* IV.299)--is dropped from Ferrier's epigraph, but it appears later in the novel in a speech by Lady Emily Lindore, niece of Lady Juliana and cousin of Juliana's daughter, Mary Douglas. The friendship and the witty but serious conversation between Mary and Lady Emily is one of the most engaging aspects of *Marriage.* It has been suggested that the two young women together make up the most accurate sketch of Ferrier's own character that we get in her novels (Bushnell 226), and indeed the conversation of Lady Emily in particular is strongly reminiscent of the intelligent, feeling, quick-witted tone of Ferrier's surviving letters. During a conversation on the nature of an ideal marriage, Mary argues the more conservative position that a woman should marry a man she can defer to and rely on for advice, while Emily argues for "a more equitable division" and criticizes men who marry foolish women so that they can more easily dominate them:

> I can detect one of these sensible husbands at a glance...who are perfect loves in their own houses--who speak their will by a nod, and lay down

the law by the motion of their eyebrow--and who attach prodigious ideas of dignity to frightening their children, and being worshipped by their wives, till you see one of these wiseacres looking as if he thought himself and his obsequious helpmate were exact personifications of Adam and Eve--he for God only, she for God in him.' Now I am much afraid, Mary, with all your sanctity, you are in some danger of becoming one of these idolatresses. (1:504-05)

Milton's orthodox Christian conviction that husbands should, by virtue of their superior reason, be spiritual guides and interpreters to their wives here becomes an anti-Christian demand that wives regard their husbands as gods in themselves. Despite Lady Emily's bantering tone, this is the closest Ferrier comes in the novel to critiquing Milton's opinion of women. Significantly, however, Lady Emily specifically denounces a male interpretation of a line that was frequently used by Ferrier's contemporaries to illustrate the inferiority of women (Wittreich xiv, 41). Her references to idolatry and pagan deities identify this response as a misreading of Milton and thus deflect criticism from the poet himself.

Throughout *Marriage* and even more in her second novel, Ferrier uses the Miltonic canon as a kind of lexicon of phrases--sometimes cliches--which add a note of hyperbole to her description of everyday events. When, after the Laird of Glenfern's death, his unreflecting relatives busy themselves with the "paraphernalia of affliction," Ferrier points out that, unlike Milton's, "[t]heir light did not 'shine inward'" (1:228). The seemingly superfluous echo of the invocation in Book III of *Paradise Lost* (111.52) nevertheless deepens the contrast between the formalities of the Glenfern household and the heroine Mary's profound emotional reaction to her grandfather's death. Mary goes into an unremitting decline which is as mysterious as it is essential to the development of the plot; her depression may strike us as melodramatic, but the Miltonic echo implies Ferrier's respect for a reaction that reveals so much more religious sensibility than everyone else's. Conversely, the dilettante and morally lax Lord Lindore is damned by Ferrier's comparison of him to Satan, when she asserts that "his was a 'mind not to be changed by place'" (1:365; cf. *PL* 1.253). The allusion is comically hyperbolic, since Lord Lindore has only left one drawing room for another. But it also foreshadows his moral corruption of his cousin Adelaide, with whom he will eventually elope, while exposing the difference between Lindore's lassitude and the fortitude that even Satan displays.

In Ferrier's second novel, *The Inheritance* (1824), the Miltonic epigraphs have almost disappeared; instead, Milton has entered more profoundly into Ferrier's prose. Not only are there more frequent verbal echoes of Milton in the text itself, but the mythological framework of *Paradise Lost* is appropriated to support the moral dimension of the novel. At an evening party, the heroine Gertrude's three cousins and suitors--Mr. Delmour, his younger brother Colonel Delmour, and Edward Lyndsay--use *Paradise Lost* to imply more than they are willing to declare about their relationship with Gertrude, while Ferrier implies more about their characters than they are willing to reveal:

'In a well-lit room there ought not to be a vestige of shade; while here, in many places, for instance where we are standing, It is absolute darkness visible.'

'Yes, It is a sort of a Pandemonium light,' said Colonel Delmour scornfully.

The mind is its own place, you know, Delmour,' said

Mr. Lyndsay; 'and in itself' he stopped and smiled.

'Go on,' cried Colonel Delmour in a voice of suppressed anger; 'pray, don't be afraid to finish your quotation.'

Mr. Lyndsay repeated, 'can make a heaven of hell, a hell of heaven.'

Colonel Delmour seemed on the point of giving way to his passion; but he checked himself; and affected to laugh, while he said—'A flattering compliment implied, no doubt; but if I am the Lucifer you insinuate, I can boast of possessing his best attributes also, for I too bear a mind not to be changed by place or time, and in my creed, constancy still ranks as a virtue.' He looked at Gertrude as he pronounced these words in an emphatic manner. (2:294)

But Colonel Delmour turns out to be a faithless lover who leads Gertrude "astray and then leaves her, Satan-like, as we are forewarned when the narrator describes his love for Gertrude as "compounded of such base materials as adversity, like the touch of Ithuriel's spear, would soon have shivered to atoms" (1:568). Adversity, in the form of Gertrude's sudden loss of her title and inheritance, indeed causes Delmour and his love to show themselves for what they are, just as the touch of the angel Ithuriel's spear in *Paradise Lost* compels the disguised Satan to reassume his true shape (*PL* IV.810-14).

The most important effect of the Miltonic undertones in *The Inheritance* is to invest the novel with a consciousness of Paradise and Hell, as well of the contrast between them, of the ease of passage from one to the other, and ultimately of the Miltonic principle that it is the mind and heart that really determine one's place, more than external circumstances. Gertrude, above all, must learn that lesson. The novel chronicles her spiritual education: she begins as the good-hearted but inexperienced and easily influenced heiress of the Earl of Rossville, accedes to the estate and title of Countess of Rossville on his death, loses everything when it is revealed that she is not really the Earl's niece but the child of a nursemaid, gains a second inheritance when her crotchety (and aptly denominated) great-uncle Adam Ramsay leaves her his estate, and regains the title of Countess when she marries the correct suitor, Edward Lyndsay, who belatedly but conveniently becomes the new heir of Rossville. As in *Marriage,* moral education is a major structural and thematic concern of the novel. The Miltonic allusions reinforce that moral purpose by giving this novel of manners cosmic overtones; that is, they underscore the spiritual significance of Ferrier's fiction as an education of the heart and soul.

When asked by her mother whether she is fond of the Rossville estate, Gertrude replies "Oh! it is Paradise to me" (2:794), and Ferrier's allusions bear out the comparison of Rossville to Eden. A string of echoes of *Paradise Lost* depicts the coming of a summer night at Rossville as an evening in Paradise: Gertrude sits at the window, "'watching the coming on of grateful evening mild'" (2:192; cf. *PL* IV.646-47) and "the deeper blue of the silent night, with her 'solemn bird and glittering stars'" (2:192; cf. *PL* IV.654-56). As in Eden or even Milton's Heaven, night "seems only a softer, sweeter day" (2:192). But the echoes of Eve's speech in Book IV of *Paradise Lost* also intensify the contrast between her unfallen confidence, as she converses with Adam, and Gertrude's anxiety, as she prepares to accompany her mother on a mysterious midnight errand to meet the sinister Lewiston, who will eventually reveal the secret of Gertrude's identity.

Early in the novel, Gertrude wanders through the Rossville landscape (described with heavy Miltonic overtones, as originally a garden of apple trees, and the image of "some ideal paradise yet to be realised"), and, like Adam in *Paradise Lost,* expresses her desire for a companion with whom to share this idyllic environment:

> 'Ah!' thought Gertrude, 'how willingly would I renounce all the pomp of greatness to dwell here in lowly affection with one who would love me, and whom I could love in return! How strange that I, who could cherish the very worm that crawls beneath my foot, have no one being to whom I can utter the thoughts of my heart--no one on whom I can bestow its best affections!' She raised her eyes, swimming in tears, to heaven; but it was in the poetical enthusiasm of feeling, not in the calm spirit of devotion. (2:109)

So Adam also petitions Heaven for a companion "fit to participate/All rational delight" (*PL* VIII.390-91) and receives Eve from God. But Gertrude, whose prayers are as yet only "poetical enthusiasm," finds no such blessed companion. Instead, in a sinister parody of the scene in *Paradise Lost,* her flawed lover Colonel Delmour immediately appears, forcing his way through the shrubbery and "hasten[ing] towards her with an appearance of the greatest delight" (2:110).

Rossville is the major inheritance in the novel, and the allusions that suggest Eden may remind us that Eden can also be considered Adam and Eve's inheritance from God, which they forfeit and must regain in a different form. The novel follows the same pattern, and Gertrude's second, regained inheritance also has Edenic overtones. This is Bloom Park, a lovely estate which is even more explicitly described as a garden and which belongs, significantly, to Uncle Adam, though he has chosen to exile himself from it. Bloom Park is first introduced to us as "such a paradise" (2:159). and Uncle Adam ironically adds, as Gertrude's vulgar cousin Bell Black is angling for Bloom Park as legacy, "I could be at nae loss for an Adam and Eve to put in it" (2:160-61). In fact, he puts Gertrude in it, arriving to take her away with him "as if Heaven-directed, at the very moment when his appearance seemed indeed as an interposition of Providence" (2:874).

But before Gertrude can resume her lost paradises "with a mind enlightened as to the true uses and advantages of power and prosperity" (2:895), she learns through a series of errors that link her, temporarily, to Satan and threaten to banish her to Hell. Entering on life with newfound wealth as Countess of Rossville when the old Earl dies, Gertrude, overwhelmed with fortune and consequence, sees her dominion as Paradise, but only from the perspective of Satan when he sneaks into Eden in order to corrupt it:

> So felt the child of prosperity, as she looked on all
> the pride of life, and, with the fallen cherub, was ready to
> exclaim--
> 0 earth, how like to heaven, if not preferr'd!' (*2:540; cf. PL* IX.99)

Worse, once Gertrude is seduced by her sudden wealth, she turns from the virtuous example of her pious aunts, "as Lucifer did from the sunbeams, only because of their brightness" (2:354; cf. *PL* IV.37). Instead of a life of steadfast virtue, Gertrude adopts flighty and unreflective schemes of philanthropy, which the narrator condemns, commenting "if schemes they might be called which plan had none" (2:541), a phrase yoking them to Milton's Death ("If shape it might be call'd that shape had none" *PL* II.667). Gertrude's virtuous cousin Anne Black, who becomes a victim of Gertrude's corrupted morals as Eve becomes a victim of Satan's, responds in the same way as Adam and Eve when they are compelled to leave Eden: "Anne dropt some natural tears, but wiped them soon" (2:542; cf. *PL* XII.645). Even Colonel Delmour, in his farewell letter to Gertrude after he determines that her inheritance is irretrievably lost, compares her unhappily to Lucifer when he refers to "that height from which you have fallen, or rather from which you have so nobly cast yourself" (2:822). Only when Gertrude has passed through a crisis of despair--beginning in a chapter headed by Adam's despondency on seeing the first terrible visions of future history (2:792; *PL* XI.763-65)--*does* she appear again as Adam or Eve with the potential to regain paradise, and Ferrier applies to her that frequently favored Romantic quotation from *Paradise Lost:* "'the world seem'd all before her where to choose'" (2:873; cf. *PL* XII.646).

All this is not to argue that *The Inheritance* is simply a rewriting of *Paradise Lost,* although that perspective would not be entirely misleading. Mary Cullinan has described *The Inheritance* as following "the traditional rise-fall-rise pattern of a *Bildungsroman*" (69), and the Miltonic echoes recall the prototype of the *Bildungsroman* in the paradise-fall-restoration pattern of Christian myth as retold by Milton. This type of reading reveals how close at hand Milton's language and his mythical and religious framework were in the early nineteenth century, not only to the canonical Romantic poets but to female writers of the novels of manners. Milton's significance for Ferrier's work reveals itself in one more way yet, in that he himself, as a writer central to both aesthetic and religious tradition, is a recurring subject of conversation among her characters. While Gertrude and her mother are staying with her pious aunts, the Miss Blacks, a musical evening turns into a discussion of religious themes in poetry and music. Miss Mary Black, the learned clergyman Mr. Z--, and Edward Lyndsay argue fervently that religious subjects bestow more lasting fame than secular ones; Mr. Lyndsay offers Milton, "undoubtedly the first poet of our country," as his primary example (2:390), and Mr. Z-- brings the debate to a stirring close by quoting a famous passage on divine inspiration from Milton's *Reason of Church-Government* (2:393; cf. Milton 671). While most modern readers will not agree with Mr. Lyndsay's and Mr. Z--'s condemnation of "profane" and "licentious" authors (including Byron, Burns, Fielding, Rousseau, and some of Shakespeare), the narrator's tone makes clear that those who prefer the religious poetry of Milton are the virtuous characters in her novel who will find their reward. The same principle holds in Ferrier's very different third novel, *Destiny* (1831), in which the heroine Edith is distinguished from her companions who fritter away Sunday afternoon reading newspapers or French plays or "playing at *spilickins*" (3:414); by contrast, we are simply told, "Edith was reading Milton" (3:415).

Ferrier's characters read and respond to Milton, and the nature of their response indicates their mental and moral capacities. The author herself uses Miltonic allusions--and the reactions to them that she may expect from her nineteenth-century readers--to focus her impulses toward both comedy and moral education. In contrast to contemporaries like Wollstonecraft and Shelley, who often reveal themselves more self-consciously as Milton's daughters, Ferrier shows a subtle creativity in adapting his myth to a semi-comic novel of everyday life, as well as a remarkable sensitivity to the witty, potentially subversive juxtaposition of his language with the manners and discourse of early nineteenth-century society.

Works Cited

Bushnell, Nelson S. "Susan Ferrier's *Marriage* as Novel of Manners." *Studies in Scottish Literature* 5(1968): 216-228.

Cullinan, Mary. *Susan Ferrier.* Boston: Hall, 1984.

Ferrier, Susan. *The Works of Susan Ferrier: Holyrood Edition.* 4 vols. London: 1929; rpt. New York: AMS, 1970.

Gilbert, Sandra M. and Susan Gubar. *The Madwoman in the Attic: The Woman Writer and the Nineteenth-Century Literary Imagination.* New Haven: Yale University Press, 1979.

Milton, John. *Complete Poems and Major Prose.* Ed. Merritt Y. Hughes. New York: Macmillan, 1957.

Parker, W. M. *Susan Ferrier and John Galt.* London: Longmans, 1965.

Paxton, Nancy L. "Subversive Feminism: A Reassessment of Susan Ferrier's *Marriage.*" *Women & Literature* 4(1976): 18-29.

Wittreich, Joseph. *Feminist Milton.* Ithaca: Cornell University Press, 1987.

Wollstonecraft, Mary. *A Vindication of the Rights of Men, A Vindication of the Rights of Woman, Hints.* Vol. 5 of *The Works of Mary Wollstonecraft.* 7 vols. Eds. Janet Todd and Marilyn Butler. London: Pickering, 1989.

The Limits of Liberal Feminism in Maria Edgeworth's *Belinda*

Kathryn Kirkpatrick

When Richard Edgeworth died in 1817, his daughter Maria took on the task of finishing his *Memoirs*. One of the details which she chose to record in her continuation of this work was her father's admiration for another woman writer, Anna Laetitia Barbauld:

> Ever the true friend and champion of female literature, and zealous for the honour of the female sex, he rejoiced with all the enthusiasm of a warm heart, when he found, as he now did, female genius guided by female discretion. He exulted in every instance of literary celebrity, supported by the amiable and respectable virtues of private life; proving by example, that the cultivation of female talents does not unfit women for their domestic duties and situation in society. (2, 259)

Here Maria Edgeworth invokes her father's approval for the model of female virtue she had consistently represented in her own work. Indeed, in her first published book, *Letters for Literary Ladies* (1795), she had argued for the compatibility, even the inseparability, of women's education, including literary activity, and the virtues of rational motherhood in the domestic realm.

Critics tend to agree that this ideal domestic woman is represented by Lady Anne Percival in Edgeworth's second novel, *Belinda* (1801). Beth Kowaleski-Wallace describes Lady Anne as a type of the "perfect mother," a model toward which the aristocratic Lady Delacour must be reformed (245). Colin and Jo Atkinson refer to her as Belinda's worthy guide, "a picture of domestic bliss surrounded by many happy children and a devoted husband" (98). Iain Topliss includes Lady Anne in a description of all the Percivals as "exemplary" but then observes, "it is the Percivals who press Belinda to marry the wrong man, and they have to eat their words" (23). Except for this small ripple, there is critical placidity over what must surely be the most striking inconsistency in the novel: *Belinda's* representative of the model woman gives the heroine what appears to be bad advice. In championing Mr. Vincent, Lady Percival endorses a suitor whom Belinda ultimately rejects in favor of Clarence Hervey, the choice of the highly flawed Lady Delacour.

I want to use this significant contradiction as a starting point for discussing the representation of a woman's proper role in the novel. In particular, I shall examine the character of Lady Anne Percival as the fictional counterpart of the rational wife and mother whom Mary Wollstonecraft advocated in *Vindication of the Rights of Woman* (1792). As a member of the Anglo-Irish gentry, Edgeworth was quite literally situated beyond the pale of the English domestic enclosure which she nonetheless helped to construct ideologically in her writing. However, Lady Percival's endorsement of the West Indian planter Mr. Vincent introduces into Edgeworth's narrative the murky colonial sources of bourgeois wealth. Although Lady Percival has much in common with the rational domestic woman that Wollstonecraft champions, her portrayal in *Belinda* also exposes the contradictions inherent in a feminism built upon the patriarchal and capitalistic foundations of liberal ideology.[1]

I

The ideal of the rational domestic woman was the staple of English Enlightenment feminism which had long maintained that the education of women in the right use of reason produced the best wives and mothers. In *Reflections on Marriage* (1706), Mary Astell argued that if "better Care [were] taken than usual in Women's Education, Marriage might recover the Dignity and Felicity of its original Institution; and Men be very happy in a married State" (15). Catherine Macaulay, in *Letters on Education* (1790), maintained that women's apparent lack of capacity for responsibility in marriage and civil society was in fact the result of their subjection to a condition of ignorance (Kirkham 11). These arguments found their fullest expression in *Vindication of the Rights of Woman* (1792) where Wollstonecraft constructs a powerful case for improvement in the status of women as ultimately in the best interests of men.

In *Vindication,* Wollstonecraft argues that the price of keeping women in a servile condition was high for both sexes. Men, she argues, exclude women from legitimate avenues of power by insisting on their status as overrefined objects of desire, and women, in turn, operate covertly as siren figures to render men themselves powerless. The right use of reason is thwarted and, for women, finds channels at the level of instinct:

> exertion of cunning is only an instinct of nature to enable them to obtain indirectly a little of that power of which they are unjustly denied a share; for, if women are not permitted to enjoy legitimate rights, they will render both men and themselves vicious to obtain illicit privileges. (89)

Here Wollstonecraft cites the exclusion of women from civil society as the condition that creates women's disruptive powers, for if women are excluded from the civil contract, they are also not bound by it--they are forced to operate as social outlaws.

For Wollstonecraft, "rights and duties are inseparable" (319) and women, deprived of the former, cannot be expected to take much interest in the latter. Genuine devotion to husbands or children becomes impossible for women schooled only in attracting and pleasing men-- they continue their enterprise for as long as their beauty lasts. Moreover, women who are undeveloped in their reason make dull companions for their husbands and negligent caretakers of their children. A vicious circle is put into place, for men who aspire to the development of their own reason render their attachment to such women obsolete. Women cannot admire what is beyond their comprehension: "how can they be expected to relish in a lover what they do not, or very imperfectly, possess themselves?" (223). Wollstonecraft concludes, "till women are led to exercise their understandings, they should not be satirized for their attachment to rakes, or even for being rakes at heart, when it appears the inevitable consequence of their education" (223).

In *Vindication,* the rational mother becomes a crucial agent in the familial circle that is the workshop for the production of new social beings. Educated herself in the right use of reason, a mother's responsibility becomes the cultivation of the same capacity in her children. She abandons the role of rival to her daughters particularly and becomes an indispensable model for children of both sexes and this without the element of coercion that Wollstonecraft sees as preparing children in the home for tyranny in the state. For parents can serve as guides only if they earn the respect of their offspring through the example of reasonable behavior; such respect cannot be had on demand. Indeed, a false subjugation of children in the home prepares them for similar relations in society: "the absurd duty, too often inculcated, of obeying a parent only on account of his being a parent, shackles the mind, and prepares it for a slavish submission to any power but reason" (268). Hence, Wollstonecraft's project for realignment of relations within the domestic realm places the reformed private self at the basis of a reformed social order. She also suggests that this social change will not come about merely by reforming women as mothers, but also by schooling men in fatherhood: "till men become attentive to the duty of a father, it is vain to expect women to spend that time in their nursery which they, 'wise in their generation,' choose to spend at their glass" (89).

Wollstonecraft has been criticized for endorsing a domestic role for middle-class women in *Vindication*. Zillah Eisenstein suggests that because this role relies on a married woman's economic dependence on her husband, it reflects Wollstonecraft's acceptance of "the liberal patriarchal world view, which distinguishes and separates male and female life--public and private" (104).[2] Yet Eisenstein also acknowledges that Wollstonecraft contradicts herself by arguing "the necessity for women's economic independence" (90). Indeed, alongside Wollstonecraft's prescriptions for domesticity in *Vindication* are her claims that marriage is often a form of prostitution because without jobs to support themselves, middle-class women have no choice but to marry for subsistence: "Business of various kinds, they might likewise pursue, if they were educated in a more orderly manner, which might save many from common and legal prostitution. Women would not then marry for a support" (261).[3]

More important for my own argument is Eisenstein's charge that although Wollstonecraft challenges the arbitrary power of hereditary rank, she nonetheless continues to support a class system in *Vindication:* "It seems that there will still be a servant class, particularly in the domestic realm. As such, Wollstonecraft's feminism seems to offer little to the wagelaboring woman" (103). And there is still less offered in *Vindication* to those colonized peoples whose exploitation (in Ireland, for instance, and the West Indies), makes possible the material affluence of bourgeois life in England.[4] As Timothy Reiss observes, Wollstonecraft is "trying to readjust the order of beneficiaries, as it were, in the dominant order. For this very reason she had no difficulty seeing other groups as candidates for exclusion" (267). These exclusions mark the limits early feminism in Britain shares with liberal ideology. And although Maria Edgeworth is generally regarded as more conservative than her feminist predecessor, her status as a woman writer in Ireland makes the social and economic relations of colonialism impossible for her to ignore. In this sense, she might be said to move beyond Wollstonecraft's formulations in *Vindication* by offering an implicit critique in *Belinda* of the blind spots in liberal feminism.

II

In *Belinda,* Edgeworth engages with the ideas Wollstonecraft put forward in *Vindication of the Rights of Woman* in several ways. Both works begin by painting negative portraits of the rakish society woman whose "gay drapery" hides social deformity; indeed the condition is manifested in *Belinda's* Lady Delacour as literal physical disease. Both *Belinda* and *Vindication* also depict the anarchic potential of woman as social outlaw; the ungovernable Mrs. Freke is represented as the source of most of the social disruption in Edgeworth's novel. Both works continue by arguing for the reform of such characters to domesticity through education in the right use of reason; in *Belinda,* Lady Delacour's cure coincides with her departure from the London public scene and her reconciliation with her husband and daughter in a setting of quiet domesticity. Finally, both works present a description of the ideal domestic woman. I want to reverse this order in my own discussion and focus not on Edgeworth's negative female types, but on the positive model toward which these characters are to be reformed. If Lady Percival is Edgeworth's ideal domestic woman, why does the reformed Lady Delacour preside at the end of the novel and why is it *her* choice of suitor whom the heroine marries?

The Percivals, as Edgeworth describes them in *Belinda,* are clearly an illustration of Wollstonecraft's enlightened, rational marriage: husband and wife share "a union of interests, occupations, taste and affections in an atmosphere of "openness" and "gaiety." At Oakly-Park, there are "no family secrets, nor any of those petty mysteries which arise from a discordance of temper or struggles for power" (196). True to Wollstonecraft's call for the ending of tyranny in the home, the Percival children are treated "neither as slaves nor as playthings, but as reasonable creatures" (196). Reigning over this picture of domestic happiness is Lady Percival whose status as an educated woman is clearly linked with her ability to perform her domestic duties to perfection:

> Lady Anne Percival had, without any pedantry or ostentation, much accurate knowledge, and a taste for literature, which made her the chosen companion of her husband's understanding, as well as of his heart. He was not obliged to reserve his conversation for friends of his own sex, nor was he forced to seclude himself in the pursuit of any branch of

> knowledge; the partner of his warmest affections was also the partner of
> his most serious occupations; and her sympathy and approbation, and the
> daily sense of her success in the education of their children, inspired him
> with a degree of happy social energy, unknown to the selfish votaries of
> avarice and ambition. (197)

Within this domestic enclosure husband and wife relate to one another
in a spirit of qualified equality, for the supportive nature of Lady
Anne's role is clearly pronounced. Yet this portrait of domestic
harmony has often been viewed uncritically. While Wollstonecraft
connects more nearly egalitarian arrangements in the home with the
end of tyranny in all its forms in civil society, Edgeworth's vision has
been said to end with the more limited goal of simple "domestic
happiness." As Iain Topliss puts this case: "The pursuit of happiness, as
Maria Edgeworth advocates it, means primarily happiness within the
present arrangements of society" (20). This assessment, however,
ignores the highly significant connections Edgeworth makes in *Belinda*
between the enlightened Percival family and the sources of their
wealth.

Clearly the influence of an educated wife keeps Mr. Percival from the
evils of the laissez faire marketplace, its atomistic isolation and
exclusive self-interest. Indeed, Mr. Percival so prefers the company of
his family that rarely in the course of the novel is he portrayed without
them. Although he is a landowner with an estate, he is never described
as managing tenants. Yet the Percivals' lifestyle depends on a particular
set of material and social relations which Edgeworth mystifies on one
level even as she reveals them on another. For, while the sources of the
Percival income are never directly discussed, the Percivals' role as
surrogate family to the West Indian Mr. Vincent connects them with
colonial wealth: "Mr. Percival, who had a regard for the father, arising
from circumstances which it is not here necessary to explain, accepted
the charge of young Vincent" (199). If we were to rewrite the sentence
to read, "Mr. Percival who had a regard for the father, arising from the
handling of an investment in a West Indian sugar plantation worked by
slaves," we can see not only why it is "not necessary here to explain"
the source of the Percivals' income, but also why it is necessary to
leave it unexplained.

On the one hand, Edgeworth's portrayal of the Percival family's
relations with Mr. Vincent is an honest attempt to own up to the
sources of bourgeois and upper-class wealth in the colonies. By
introducing Mr. Vincent into the domestic haven at Oakly-Park,
Edgeworth was allotting a colonial the social status that his economic

position seems to demand. On the other hand, Mr. Vincent's very presence in the novel undermines the legitimacy of the family circle he joins. The plantation system in the West Indies relied on one of the most brutal examples of chattel slavery in human history, and Mr. Vincent is from precisely the planter class that enacted the system. What Edgeworth's narrative thus reveals is an implicit recognition of the compromised position of her model domestic family. In what sense, her narrative essentially asks, is Wollstonecraft's rational bourgeois wife and mother in complicity with these social and economic relations?

Although the issue is dauntingly thorny, I would argue that Edgeworth is struggling with the question of collusion in systems of colonial oppression in *Belinda* and that her novel sees beyond the obviously implicated English patriarch and his dark twin, the enacting colonizer, to the role of the bourgeois wife. As I have suggested, Edgeworth has some understanding of the condition of both colonizers and colonized; while she appears to belong to the Anglo-Irish gentry, her legal and economic status as a woman gives her a kinship with the disenfranchised Irish Catholics. Indeed, she chooses to narrate her first novel, *Castle Rackrent,* through the voice of an Irish Catholic steward. Moreover, the influence of her immediate family, particularly her father, in her formative years sets her intellectually at odds with the whole colonizing process in Ireland. Richard Edgeworth made his debut in the newly independent Irish Parliament in 1782 with a speech arguing for extending the franchise to Catholic freeholders (*Memoirs,* 2, 51), a gesture that marked the beginning of his estrangement for two decades from other Protestants in Ireland. Yet as Albert Memmi argues in *The Colonizer and the Colonized,* no member of a colonizing class, however benevolent toward the indigenous population, can avoid complicity with the colonial system of oppression because "all Europeans in the colonies are privileged" (10). The colonial, "whether he expressly wishes it or not, is received as a privileged person by the institutions, customs and people" (17).

Although her gender leaves her without a direct stake in colonial transactions, that she can generate such a massive canon attests to a belief in a woman writer's ability to influence social perceptions, behavior, and values. She would not have viewed herself or other women of her class as dispossessed victims, however much her experience teaches her to understand that condition. And if a woman can be an agent, albeit in an indirect or supporting role, she can also be responsible for the outcomes she helps to influence. This is the lesson that Edgeworth's first full fictional portrayal of the ideal domestic woman, Lady Percival, demonstrates in *Belinda.*

As "the partner of his most serious occupations," Lady Percival supports on a social level what her husband enacts on a financial one: she urges Mr. Vincent's suit while Mr. Percival borrows Mr. Vincent's money. But once Mr. Percival can no longer rely on his former ward's income and Belinda has rejected Mr. Vincent's offer of marriage, Lady Percival is forced to retreat while Mr. Vincent departs for the continent:

> Lady Anne Percival, in a very kind and sensible letter, expressed the highest approbation of Belinda's conduct; and the most sincere hope that Belinda would still continue to think of her with affection and esteem, though she had been so rash in her advice, and though her friendship had been apparently so selfish. (407)

This is an odd exit for one who is in all other respects presented as the novel's most exemplary woman. Here Lady Percival admits to having given bad advice out of her own self interest. Thus, Edgeworth's heroine cannot entirely rely on the judgment of her ideal domestic woman. That woman, her novel demonstrates, is not as politically disinterested as she appears. She is, in fact, tied to her economic base in ways that influence both her perceptions and her decisions. It is one of the ways in which liberal feminism remained shortsighted.

Edgeworth addresses this dilemma in the conclusion of *Belinda* by giving Lady Delacour, the reformed aristocrat, precedence. In the final scene, Lady Delacour adopts the role of stage manager and arranges the novel's characters in a tableau of appropriate couplings: the West Indians, Virginia and Captain Sunderland; the landed aristocrats, Lord and Lady Delacour; and the gentry, Mr. Hervey and Belinda. The Percivals are conspicuous by their absence as is Mr. Vincent, for the novel has failed to integrate them and their West Indian incomes fully into the social fabric it represents. The remaining West Indian characters marry each other, thereby maintaining an endogamous social unit. These self-reflexive gestures in the closing pages underscore the novel's lack of resolution, quite literally, by acknowledging the ending as "staged." Lady Delacour presides, the heiress with old, untainted money newly reformed to bourgeois domesticity. Edgeworth offers her as the alternative ideal woman even as she acknowledges this newly proffered choice as fictive.

Works Cited

Astell, Mary. *Some Reflections Upon Marriage*. 1730. New York: Source Book
    Press, 1970.
Atkinson, Colin B. and Jo Atkinson. "Maria Edgeworth, Belinda, and Women's
    Rights." *Eire-Ireland: A Journal of Irish Studies* 19.4(1984): 94-118.
Edgeworth, Maria. *Belinda*. 1810 3rd ed. London: Pandora Press, 1986.
Edgeworth, Richard Lovell. *Memoirs of Richard Lovell Edgeworth
    Begun by Himself and Concluded by has Daughter Maria
    Edgeworth*. 2 vols. 1820. Shannon, Ireland: Irish University Press,
    1969.
Eisenstein, Zillah. *The Radical Future of Liberal Feminism*. New York:
    Longmans, 1981.
Kirkham, Margaret. *Jane Austen, Feminism and Fiction*. New York Methuen:
    1983.
Kowaleski-Wallace, Beth. "Home Economics: Domestic Ideology in Maria
    Edgeworth's *Belinda*." *The Eighteenth-Century: Theory and
    Interpretation* 29(1988): 242-262.
Memmi, Albert. *The Colonizer and the Colonized*. Boston: Beacon Press, 1965.
Reiss, Timothy J. *The Meaning of Literature*. Ithaca: Cornell University Press,
    1992.
Topliss, Iain. "Mary Wollstonecraft and Maria Edgeworth's Modern
    Ladies." *Etudes Irlandaises* 6(1981): 13-31.
Wollstonecraft, Mary. *Vindication of the Rights of Woman*. 1792. New York:
    Penguin, 1798.

Endnotes

[1] Zillah Eisenstein defines liberal ideology as "the specific set of ideas that developed with the bourgeois revolution asserting the importance and autonomy of the individual" (4). Developing in England in the 17th century and firmly in place by the 19th, this ideology supported the dominance of the bourgeois male in part by promoting his financial self-interest through the economic practice of capitalism--exploitation of wage laborers within England and brutalization of slaves and peasants in the colonies of the West Indies and Ireland. Critics like Eisenstein and Cora Kaplan ("Pandora's Box: Subjectivity, Class and Sexuality in Socialist Feminist Criticism" in *Feminisms*, ed. Robyn R. Warhol and Diane Price Herndl, New Brunswick: Rutgers UP, 1991) warn that in claiming the emancipatory moments of this ideology for women we must avoid the danger of creating a liberal feminism that reproduces racial and class oppression.

[2] Timothy Reiss makes a similar point when he observes that by arguing her case within the dominant discourse of liberalism, Wollstonecraft is forced "to make motherhood the primary function of women as social beings, as 'citizens,' despite her own actual and stated experience of the subordinate

status this inevitably imposed on women" (277).

³ Wollstonecraft makes this critique of marriage explicit in *Maria or the Wrongs of Woman* where she portrays a brutish husband who tries to pay off a debt to a friend by offering his wife's sexual favors. Later, in the final courtroom scene, Maria argues that true chastity is often violated in marriage.

⁴ For a more thorough discussion of the West Indian characters in *Belinda*, see my "'Gentlemen Have Horrors Upon This Subject': West Indian Suitors in Maria Edgeworth's *Belinda*" (*Eighteenth-Century Fiction*, 5 [1993]: 331-481).

"Did the Warwickshire militia...teach the Irish to drink beer, or did they learn from the Irish to drink whiskey?":
A Reading of Maria Edgeworth's *Castle Rackrent*[1]

David W. Ullrich

Maria Edgeworth deserves inclusion in representations of Romanticism because her work articulates the conflicting liberal and conservative impulses of late eighteenth-century rationalism and yet remains relevant to contemporary critical inquiries. In *Castle Rackrent* Edgeworth represents language as politically charged and culturally determined and incorporates the oblique narrative style and historical episodes of *The Black Book of Edgeworthstown,* illustrating that the packaging of narrative and history is important to dissemination. Edgeworth's recognition of the futility of strict demarcations between fictive and historical constructions is encoded in the tellingly awkward subtitle of *Castle Rackrent:* "An Hibernian Tale Taken from Facts, and from the Manners of the Irish Squires, Before the Year 1782." Moreover, the narrative strategy of *Castle Rackrent* eschews presenting conflicting cultural debates filtered through the emotional excess of autobiography, providing a healthy alternative to masculinist Romanticism. *Castle Rackrent's* multi-framed, multivocal narrative effaces unity and, instead, inscribes competing interpretations. The interpolated narrative structure of *Castle Rackrent* combines Edgeworth's rationalistic efforts to represent the speech acts of Thady Quirk as objective with a Romantic interpretation emphasizing the figural and contextual nature of those speech acts.

Castle Rackrent analyzes how language, custom, law, family, and narrative itself all perpetuate competing forms of cultural identity (for scholarship, see Owens). This cultural contest, thematized by the

Anglo-Irish conflict, is inscribed in the narrative through various competitions between language systems; between dominant, foreign law and indigenous, minority culture and customs; between heavily positioned historiography; and between male ascendancy and women's and children's rights. *Castle Rackrent's* self-conscious, "quirky" narrative deftly ensnares the reader in these battles. At stake in the contested space of the narrative is a claim for originary status and, hence, ultimate authority as to who should inhabit the castle, who constitutes the family to whom Thady Quirk wants to remain loyal. Finally, in *Castle Rackrent,* cultures are incommensurable, spouses cannot procreate, narratives collapse into silence.

Castle Rackrent configures language as difference and narrative as contested space. Before the narrative begins, Edgeworth inserts a framing Preface justifying her narrative technique and its vernacular idiom and chastising her implied audience: "the *ignorant* [later, *"lazy"* (11, n. 100)] English reader" (4, Edgeworth's italics).[2] Specifically, *Castle Rackrent* configures language as a false opposition between Irish idiom and culture and English legalese. Irish culture and idiom are expressed as originary through genealogy (the O'Shauglin/Rackrents presented as a disjointed, achronological muddle), through proper names and place names (O'Neills of Ballynagrotty, Moneygawls of Mount Juliet's Town, and O'Shannons of New Town Tullyhog), and through customs (whillaluh, raking pot of tea, wake), mythologies (fairy-mount, banshee) and idiomatic speech acts ("he never lost one-- but seventeen" and distinctions between "kilt" and "killed"). These elements represent Irish culture as an indigenous, coherent system of signification, however eccentric or mystifying it might appear to an outsider. Indeed, the implied readership is positioned as just such an outsider, equally puzzled by Irish customs, by the narrator's relationship to this complex linguistic and cultural system of signification, and by the accompanying editorial footnotes and gloss notes, commenting explicitly on this system and implicitly on the insufficient and contested nature of narrative.[3] Scores of idioms, intrusive asides, footnotes, and glossary notes waylay the reader in a contentious textual fabric of the novel's competing constituents and audiences: rural Irish, Anglo-Irish ascendancy, and Regency London. The reader gradually understands that the choice between O'Shauglin and Rackrent is inextricably entangled within larger political, religious, and economic choices. Eventually, nothing is taken at face value, least of all Thady's statement, "as I have lived so will I die, true and loyal to the family" (8).

These Irish claims are opposed by the Anglo-Irish ascendancy's claim, represented in the legalistic expressions associated with Sir Murtagh and his wife. "Duty fowl," "duty geese," "weed ashes," "sealing money," "privy purse," "glove money," and other euphemisms refer to customs, presented as originary by virtue of feudal tradition and legal codification, amounting to extortion. The editor explains these euphemisms and their histories in footnotes and gloss notes under the pretext that such acts of domination no longer occur, although the notes clearly indict the Anglo-Irish absentee gentry.

Thus, the act of reading *Castle Rackrent* becomes a series of choices between alternative language systems; between idiom, ritual, myth, or law; and between alternative narratives, the primary narrative or the (literally) marginalized narrative of footnote or gloss note. In a *tour de force* of cultural verisimilitude, Edgeworth inscribes English representations of history as more easily accessible, easily understandable, and, therefore, likely to be transmitted to future generations as received. A secondary narrative inscribes Irish representations as in competition with the former and yet less accessible and more obscure and quirky, and, therefore, likely to be marginalized. Edgeworth, as editor, carefully shifts her allegiances between factions, between narratives, reflecting her own double position. She sympathizes with the Irish as an oppressed people but suspects the very myths and customs that bedazzle and entertain. Similarly, Edgeworth values English reason but opposes its repressive misuse as feudal law or formative nationalism.

The frequency of these textual skirmishes results in a hypertext, effectively recreating the day-to-day linguistic, cultural, and political tensions between rural Irish and Anglo-Irish ascendancy. In turn, these tensions sensitize the reader, cautioning one to read literally between the lines, to become attentive to the political nuances of language, and to view any narrative or history as a heavily invested, positioned story. In the act of reading the history of Castle Rackrent, one becomes, like Thady at closure, confused, exhausted, silent. The competing systems--one expressive, Gaelic, and mythic, the other referential, English, and litigious--reach a stalemate. One must look beyond this false opposition to find a perspective consonant with Edgeworth's rationalism.

Edgeworth realized felicitously that a conventional omniscient narrator positioned outside of and pitted against a sequence of Rackrent heirs would not enable her to reconstruct this interwoven, intensely provincial dialectic of suspicion and hatred. Thady Quirk as narrator occupies the pivotal position as insider and outsider, as separate from but dependent upon the Rackrent estate (see Owens). Wily, ironic, and ambivalent in his complex narrative voice, Thady Quirk remains sufficiently superficial and provincial in his understanding to require an editor to (further) interpolate the various contexts of Castle Rackrent. However, Thady's double position, implied culpability, and tonal ambivalence hamstring his possibilities as a character who can represent the Anglo-Irish gentry's barbaric treatment of the rural Irish which Edgeworth witnessed. Moreover, Edgeworth understands that granting Thady's character such a sympathetic position would privilege Irish claims over English. Edgeworth needs to inscribe minority persecution without reference to the totalized, claustrophobic English and Irish positions. Moreover, since language itself is figured in *Castle Rackrent* as always already positioned, Edgeworth's character must remain a silent signifier, a voiceless voice.

Such a universal example of minority victimization is represented by Sir Kit's wife, Lady Rackrent, first presented, appropriately, through her speech acts.[4] When Sir Kit and the unnamed "Jew Lady Rackrent" (37) arrive at the castle, a series of linguistic skirmishes sets "the corner stone for all her future misfortunes," as Thady tells it (28). Lady Rackrent inquires about a "pile of black bricks," which Sir Kit informs her is "my turf stack." She then "takes out her glass," and as Thady interpolates, "begins spying over the country," inquiring about "that black swamp," "a very ugly prospect" (27).[5] "My bog," as Kit calls it, is a landmark for the Rackrents, recalling the original, forsaken family name and Sir Murtagh's embittered litigation to retain the property. When Thady mentions its name--Allyballycarrick'oshaughlin--Lady Rackrent "fell to laughing like one out of their right mind," makes Thady repeat the name "a dozen times," "must ask me how to spell it," and asks [of all things] "what was the meaning of it in English" (28). Initially, these indelicacies cause Thady to view Lady Rackrent unsympathetically. They also embarrass the hot-blooded Sir Kit, publicly illustrating that he, like his ancestors, has married for money.

I suggest that Lady Rackrent--as woman and Jew--reinscribes the issue of Irish-Catholic minority status in a more universal context.[6] Through Lady Rackrent, Edgeworth critiques the male-dominated Anglo-Irish ascendancy's attempts to balance race and religion with affluence in valuing a woman's marital eligibility. Lady Rackrent's physiognomy and complexion are described by Thady as identifiably "other": as "blackamoor," "heretic Blackamoor," and "Nabob" (25, 26)--peoples, like the Jews, with uneasy historical, political, and religious relationships with England.[7] Her "dark complexion" (26) is

"stale-mates" between Sir Murtagh and Lady Rackrent, Sir Kit and his Lady, and Sir Condy and Lady Isabella. As to unitary law or totalized representations of truth: "the memorandum not being on stamped paper, some say it is worth nothing, others again it may do; others say, Jason won't have the lands at any rate--many wishes it so..." (96).

Edgeworth's postscript to *Castle Rackrent*--which heads this chapter--underscores her realization that she could not resolve the issues presented in *Castle Rackrent* through the narrative or within her rationalistic program. Her appreciation for the novel's ingenious narrative along with her understanding of the changing historical particulars in Ireland explain amply why she wisely refused to write a sequel. Instead, she recasts these issues in the more manageable narrative structures of her other Irish novels, *Ennui* (1809), *The Absentee* (1812), and *Ormond* (1817). However, I want to suggest briefly that an alternative, more hopeful conclusion to *Castle Rackrent* exists in Edgeworth's *The Parent's Assistant* (1793-1796, 1800), written before *Castle Rackrent* and significantly expanded contemporaneously with its composition.

The Parent's Assistant can be read as an idealistic preface to *Castle Rackrent*. The formidable issues in *Castle Rackrent* have been resolved in theory in the idealized landscape of *The Parent's Assistant,* where an industrious work ethic, social egalitarianism, intelligent women, and integration of familial and societal values through children triumph over family ignorance and sloth, racial prejudice, and local myth and custom conflicting with feudal law. One representative story, "Forgive and Forget," serves as a prescient example of the wished-for resolution to *Castle Rackrent.* Mr. Oakly, self-described as "a plain, *unlearned* Englishman" (223, Edgeworth's italics), is suspicious of his neighbor, Mr. Grant, because Mr. Grant is a Scotchman and not a "true-born Englishman" (222) like himself. Mr. Oakly's prejudice profoundly disrupts the two families' affectionate, even productive, relationship. Maurice and "Arthur," like their respective fathers, tend gardens. Mr. Grant and Maurice produce the best and largest "Brobdignag" raspberries by scientific farming techniques (237-38) and the best tulips, significantly, by crossbreeding (246). The motivation for telling the story comes from Mr. Oakly's misinterpretation of an interpolated account of a narrative between Mrs. Oakly and Mrs. Grant (225-26). However, in "Forgive and Forget," acts of interpolation are kept out of the text, subordinated to a conventional, omniscient narrative better suited to a tidy, morally unambiguous resolution.

The story's subplots reinforce the idea of "Forgive and Forget" as posing preconceived, theoretical solutions to the linguistic, cultural, and narratological problems in *Castle Rackrent*. These subplots include conflict between local custom and legalistic efforts to overrule custom (231-32); belief in the efficacy of law, linked ironically to English nationalism (233); bribes offered for potential favors (243); and racial stereotypes presented as misguided and prejudiced. These obstacles are overcome by Edgeworth's program of education for children: *"book-larning"* (250, Edgeworth's italics). The story's conclusion stresses that children who read will become informed, overcome cultural prejudice, and prosper through scientific agriculture. One wishes the allegorical conclusion of "Forgive and Forget" could be grafted onto *Castle Rackrent:* "The two boys rejoiced in this family union" (251). The perceptive reader understands that Edgeworth employs an overwritten, clichéd morality in order to make palatable to her audience a keen-edged social criticism thought radical in her day. *The Parent's Assistant* offers tentative, theoretical solutions--in an idealized landscape and through a manageable narrative structure--to the pragmatic linguistic and cultural problems of *Castle Rackrent.*

In closing, I would cast Maria Edgeworth not only as an early Romantic but also as an incipient Victorian in an effort to emphasize her prophetic vision. Embedded in *Castle Rackrent* are the social and political issues of Disraeli's *Sybil,* the self-conscious use of history and narrative in Carlyle's *Sartor Resartus,* and the brilliant use of idiom as characterization found throughout Dickens. We need to re-evaluate Maria Edgeworth's entire oeuvre, not only *Castle Rackrent,* but her other fiction, her children's stories and her substantial nonfiction for what they tell us about the various contexts of early Romanticism.

Works Cited

Butler, Marilyn. *Maria Edgeworth: A Literary Biography.* Oxford: Clarendon, 1972.

Edgeworth, Maria. *Castle Rackrent: An Hibernian Tale Taken from Facts, and from the Manners of the Irish Squires, before the Year 1782.* 1800; rpt. Ed. George Watson. Oxford: Oxford University Press, 1990.

___. *The Parent's Assistant; or, Stories for Children.* 1800. 6 vols. Selected and arranged by Alison Lurie and Justin G. Schiller. New York: Garland, 1976.

Edgeworth, Richard Lovell, and Maria Edgeworth. *Essay on Irish Bulls.* 1802. Selected by Robert Lee Wolff. New York: Garland, 1978.

Harden, Elizabeth. *Maria Edgeworth.* Boston: Twayne, 1984.

Kowaleski-Wallace, Elizabeth. *Their Fathers' Daughters: Hannah More,*

Maria Edgeworth, and Patriarchal Complicity. Oxford: Oxford University Press, 1991.

McCormack, W. J., and Kim Walker. "Introduction." *The Absentee*. By Maria Edgeworth. Oxford: Oxford University Press, 1988. ix-xlii.

Newman, Peter R. "Black List." *Companion to Irish History 1603-1921, From the Submission of Tyrone to Partition.* Oxford: Facts on File, 1991.

Owens, Cóilín. *Family Chronicles: Maria Edgeworth's Castle Rackrent.* Gen. Ed. Maurice Harmon. Dublin: Wolfhound Press, 1987.

Edgar. "The Jew in Western Drama: An Essay and a Checklist." *The Jew in English Drama: An Annotated Bibliography.* Comp. by Edward D. Coleman. New York: New York Public Library, 1970. 1-50.

Salces, Juan E. Tazón. "Politics, Literature, and Colonization: A View of Ireland in the Sixteenth Century." *The Clash of Ireland: Literary Contrasts and Connections.* Eds. C.C. Barfoot and Theo D'haen. Amsterdam: Rodopi, 1989. 23-36.

Endnotes

[1] Time for this essay was made available through a sabbatical from Birmingham-Southern College. I wish to thank Janice Poplau and the Inter-library Loan staff for their efforts and patience. Thanks, also, to Professors Ashe, Lester, and Murphy-Ullrich.

[2] Edgeworth's Preface shares many ideas with Wordsworth's Preface to *Lyrical Ballads*, specifically, that "anecdote" and the "careless conversations" of "a gossip" are psychologically transparent, approximate truth (1-3).

[3] Edgeworth's first footnote is emblematic of her implied critique against representations of history or narrative as capable of occupying originary status. Embedded deep within the dissertation on Thady's greatcoat and its history, the editor corrects an English misnomer, changing Spenser's "thick woods" from *A Vewe of the Present State of Ireland* to "black bogs" (7—8 and n., Edgeworth's italics), thus challenging English views of Ireland.

[4] Edgeworth's perceived anti-Semitism, her Jewish characterizations, and her letters to Rachel Mordecai have been addressed (Butler 238, Harden 87-88, McCormack and Walker xv-xviii).

[5] Thady Quirk's implication that Lady Rackrent is "spying," coupled with Lady Rackrent's repeating "black," suggests subtly Edgeworth's irony for her family's position toward the Anglo-Irish question. "The Black List" was a "schedule of those members of the Irish Parliament who were accused of selling Ireland to the union with Britain, In return for personal profit and preferment" ("Black List"). See Butler 111-14, 136-41, 181-84, and 202-03 on this and related topics.

[6] In the early 1800s, Catholic emancipation dovetailed with Jewish emancipation, as Byron notes in attacking anti-Catholic prejudice (qtd. in McCormack and Walker xi). Similarly, Rosenberg notes that Jews and the black complexioned were lumped together as stage types before and during this .time period (39).

[7] In 1290, Edward I expelled all Jews from England; Jews were not readmitted until Cromwell did so in the 1650s. Recall the then-current debates over abolition of slavery and Indian colonization.

[8] For an examination of the connection between Black (haired) Irish and (dark-haired) Spanish, see Salces on the "legend . recorded by a good number of writers" including Spenser, "of the Spanish foundation of Ireland"(24) and its political and religious implications in the sixteenth century. Further speculation on late eighteenth century political contexts of "black" notes, with respect to the Irish, the metonymy in "black bogs" and Black Irish, the offspring of interracial marriage between transported Irish and West Indian women being called Black Irish; with respect to the Indian, the "black hole of Calcutta" Incident in 1756; and with respect to "blackamoor," the allusions to Othello.

[9] The history of such power relationships is perhaps best summarized in Walpole's neologism "to nugentise," meaning to marry successive rich women. See McCormack and Walker (xxv).

[10] As Watson notes, Edgeworth has Sir Kit allude to Lady Rack-rent as "my pretty Jessica" (31, 122 n.), Shylock's daughter in *Merchant of Venice*. The allusion foregrounds race, the economics of womanhood, dominant and marginalized cultures, and the suspicions facing a (converted) Jewish woman in a Christian community.

[11] Moreover, in *Essay on Irish Bulls*, Richard and Maria Edgeworth explode any unitary notion of the English language, listing several dialects (9), illustrating how signification of a signified is context-specific and culturally determined (4-5), and in a brilliant parody of etymological "proofs," positing that "Irish bulls" may be derived from papal bull, John Bull, bullhead (16-8). With specific reference to the Anglo-Irish question, the Edgeworths subvert the notion of English linguistic supremacy. In a tongue-in-cheek argument, they allege that the English came to Ireland during the time of Elizabeth and Shakespeare, and since Ireland remained in relative geographic isolation, "their vocabulary has been preserved nearly in its pristine purity" (200). Thus, the Irish retain a pure and proper Elizabethan English and notions of originary language are turned topsy-turvy.

[12] The song, from John Fletcher's *The Bloody Brother; or. Rollo. Duke of Normandy* is ironic. Soon after it is sung, Rollo kills his brother Otto. *The Bloody Brother* was often excerpted at this time (see Leigh Hunt's *Selections*

from the Works of Beaumont and Fletcher).

[13] Edgeworth's allusions to *Othello* and the *Merchant of Venice* point to racial mistrust, religious and economic suspicions, and nationalistic conflict as issues in *Castle Rackrent.*

Mary Wollstonecraft and
Mary Shelley: Ideological Affinities

William D. Brewer

> By allowing women but one way of rising in the
> world, the fostering [of] the libertinism of men,
> society makes monsters of them, and then their
> ignoble vices are brought forward as a proof of
> inferiority of intellect.
>
> --Wollstonecraft, *The Wrongs of Woman* (137)

Although many critics have viewed Mary Shelley as "the
conservative daughter of a radical mother" (Sunstein 7), a comparison
of her fiction to the works of Mary Wollstonecraft reveals that Shelley
shared her mother's belief that women were victimized by "a false
system of education" (*Vindication* 7).[1] According to Mary Poovey,
"Shelley's one unqualified affirmation about herself is that she accepts
the conventional wisdom especially pertinent to female education: life
is a school of instructive negation; a woman matures by disciplining
and denying herself" (115). Shelley's own education went, however,
far beyond "instructive negation": she received from her father,
William Godwin, an education that Wollstonecraft would have approv-
ingly called "masculine," an education which covered ancient and
modern history, literature, and Latin (see *Vindication* 77; Sunstein 39-
41).[2] It was an education that Shelley was later to celebrate in her novel
Valperga, in which Euthanasia, the novel's heroine, is painstakingly
instructed by her doting father: "The effect of this education on her
mind was advantageous and memorable; she did not acquire that
narrow idea of the present times, as if they and the world were the
same, which characterizes the unlearned; she saw and marked the
revolutions that had been" (1: 28-29). Having been provided an

excellent liberal arts background by her father, Shelley went on to read and reread her mother's works, which describe the false system of feminine education that continued to victimize her contemporaries. Of course Shelley, unlike her mother, never became a polemical writer seeking social reforms, but her attitudes toward education, especially the education of women, are reflected in her works and bear the unmistakable stamp of her mother's influence.

As Tayler and Luria point out in "Gender and Genre: Women in British Romantic Literature," one of the chief problems faced by women writers during the Romantic period was their exclusion from a classical education: "Far more debilitating for women even than their legal status--at least from the point of view of the history of literature-- was the poverty and narrowness of their education, especially their systematic exclusion from training in the classics." Since Latin, the language used in the learned professions, was taught only to boys, "the main body of learning, content as well [as] technique, was transmitted in a language and literature not available to women" (100). Wollstonecraft, whose formal training was limited to a day school in Yorkshire, where "she learned little more than reading and writing," evidently felt that her "feminine" education did not adequately prepare her for a career as a professional writer (Tomalin 21). In *A Vindication of the Rights of Women,* Wollstonecraft longs for schools in which girls would receive the same educational opportunities afforded boys: "The young people of superior abilities, or fortune, might...be taught [after the age of nine] the dead and living languages, the elements of science, and continue the study of history and politics, on a more extensive scale, which would not exclude polite literature. Girls and boys still together? I hear some readers ask: yes" (168). But during Wollstonecraft's and Shelley's lifetimes, women were not allowed into the fraternity of educated men even when, as in the case of Anna Laetitia Barbauld, they were given a classical education. As Tayler and Luria note, "the result for Anna was intellectual isolation, for her brother was educated away from home and she was herself kept carefully apart from the schoolboys" (103). The need for coeducation was obvious to Wollstonecraft, who in *A Vindication* argues "that to improve both sexes they ought, not only in private families, but in public schools, to be educated together" (165), and Shelley, who spent much of her married life studying literature, languages, and philosophy with Percy Shelley, would certainly have agreed with this declaration.

Although Shelley's fiction does not make overt demands for social and political change, it often confronts the problems caused by the inadequate education of women. As Janet Todd has shown, even *Frankenstein,* which focuses on male characters, is influenced by Wollstonecraft's feminist concerns: the monster's plight as a self-educated outcast has resemblances to the condition of Jemima, the fallen woman of Wollstonecraft's *The Wrongs of Woman.* As Todd argues, "Like the monster, the woman is separated by her physical condition from the dominant male society and--in the case of the fallen woman--from the family as well" (18-19). The lower-class Jemima and the monster must educate themselves, and in both cases their efforts to educate themselves are nothing less than heroic. While Jemima receives her education as the mistress of a "literary man" who allows her to hear "discussions, from which, in the common course of life, women are excluded" (113, 111), the monster learns to speak by observing Felix as he instructs Safie. These secondhand educations lead to dissatisfaction rather than happiness. After the sudden death of Jemima's gentleman lover, she must return to isolation and poverty: "I had acquired a taste for literature, during the five years I had lived with a literary man, occasionally conversing with men of the first abilities of the age; and now to descend to the lowest vulgarity, was a degree of wretchedness not to be imagined unfelt" (113). Likewise, the monster's education only serves to underscore his wretchedness: "Was I then a monster, a blot upon the earth, from which all men fled, and whom all men disowned? I cannot describe to you the agony that these reflections inflicted upon me; I tried to dispel them, but sorrow only increased with knowledge" (89). Like Jemima, the monster is denied a place in society or within a family, and education serves only to make his intolerable situation even more painfully clear.

The incomplete and unsatisfying educations of Jemima and the monster lead, in part, to their sociopathic behaviors. Jemima describes how she indirectly caused a pregnant woman's death by having her lover turn the woman out. Jemima's regret following the woman's tragic demise foreshadows the monster's remorse in *Frankenstein* after the death of his creator, especially when she exclaims: "I thought of my own state, and wondered how I could be such a monster!" (*The Wrongs of Woman* 116). A male-dominated society has made Jemima into a monster, just as a male creator gives life to a monster in *Frankenstein*--in both cases, there is a failure to nurture and educate the disadvantaged. It is significant, moreover, that Shelley's monster echoes a declaration from the conclusion of *A Vindication.* Wollstonecraft's "Let woman share the rights and she will emulate the virtues of man" (194) can be compared to the monster's plea to

Frankenstein: "Make me happy, and I shall again be virtuous" (74). The monster, like women (especially fallen women), has become vicious partly because he has never been provided with the opportunities that he has a right to expect. Thus one could argue that Frankenstein's failure to educate and guide the newly created monster is, by extension, an indictment of a society which would allow a woman like Jemima to be brutalized, raped, and forced to earn a living as a prostitute, while at the same time spurning her as a "monster."

But while *The Wrongs of Woman* and *Frankenstein* reflect on the educations of characters who are without families, in Shelley's *Mathilda*, which is heavily influenced by Wollstonecraft, the title character has a family, including a father whose passion for her and subsequent suicide drive her to the edge of madness. The first draft of what was to become *Mathilda*, entitled *The Fields of Fancy*, was inspired by Wollstonecraft's *Cave of Fancy*, both of which present moral lessons within a visionary context. In *Cave of Fancy* a sage named Sagestus rescues a young girl who has been orphaned by a shipwreck. Sagestus does not regard the death of the girl's mother as a tragedy, since he judges that the mother, who was apparently corrupted by "an improper education," would probably have proved an unfit guardian for the child (197). The remainder of the unfinished *Cave of Fancy* was to have consisted of a series of moral lessons delivered by spirits in Sagestus's visionary cave, lessons designed to provide the girl (whom Sagestus names Sagesta) with a proper education. The only one of these educational tales completed by Wollstonecraft is delivered by an anonymous female spirit, who tells Sagesta how she conquered her passion for a married man. Like Shelley's Mathilda, who longs to be reunited with her father in death (244), the spirit "silently anticipate[s] the happiness she should enjoy" when she will encounter the spirit of the man she loved in the afterlife (202). There is clearly a necrophiliac element in both *Mathilda* and *Cave of Fancy*.

But although the *Cave of Fancy* resembles Shelley's *Fields of Fancy* in its visionary form and educational intent, the unfinished tales also have important differences. While Wollstonecraft is concerned with the education of a young girl by an old man, Shelley presents a mature woman who, having suffered a misfortune that reduced [her] to misery and despair," is instructed by "the Prophetess Diotima the instructress of Socrates" (90, 94). Although Shelley would surely have agreed with Wollstonecraft that an old sage is an appropriate tutor for a young girl (Godwin's education of Shelley comes immediately to mind), *The Fields of Fancy* suggests that an adult woman needs female guidance, and in Shelley's novel *Valperga,* begun before and finished after *Mathilda,* only Euthanasia can comfort the traumatized Beatrice. In fact, in *Mathilda,* the older man, Mathilda's father, is the reason for her sorrows: rather than preparing her to face life, his confession of his incestuous passion for her and his subsequent suicide make it virtually impossible for her to live, either in society or in seclusion. He is a dysfunctional opposite of the wise Sagestus, whose goal is to give Sagesta a proper education before she rejoins the outside world.

Thus although in *Cave of Fancy* the father figure Sagestus is presented as a preferable alternative to Sagesta's weak and prejudiced mother, *Mathilda* describes the evil effects that result when, after the death of his wife, a father neglects and then fatally misdirects his daughter. Of course, one advantage Sagestus has over Mathilda's father and Sagesta's mother is that he is not a parent. Because he is not related to Sagesta, he can be more objective in his dealings with her. Like the governor of Rousseau's *Emile,* he can educate his pupil without being drawn into the emotional conflicts that plague many parent-child relationships. Both *Cave of Fancy* and *Mathilda* suggest that parents are sometimes the worst educators of their children, and in this they are consistent with Rousseau's principles.

But although the initial version of *Mathilda* grew out of Wollstone-craft's *Cave of Fancy,* the finished novella is much closer to Wollstonecraft's *Mary, A Fiction,* especially since both *Mathilda* and *Mary* explore the development of women who are neglected by their parents throughout their childhoods. As Wollstonecraft writes in *Vindication,* "A great proportion of the misery that wanders, in hideous forms, around the world, is allowed to rise from the negligence of parents" (154). Growing up in dreamworlds, these protagonists experience extreme disillusionment when they are faced with the vicissitudes of life and spend their later years in states of chronic depression. And for neither Wollstonecraft's Mary nor Shelley's Mathilda is there a strong maternal guide for their childhood years. Mary's mother Eliza "was educated with the expectation of a large fortune, [and] of course became a mere machine: the homage of her attendants made a great part of her puerile amusements, and she never imagined there were any relative duties for her to fulfil" (1). Sickly and delicate, Eliza whiles away the time by reading "those most delightful substitutes for bodily dissipation, novels" (2). Although she is fond of her son, Eliza's relationship to Mary is marked by repulsion and neglect: "when Mary, the little blushing girl, appeared, she would send the awkward thing away" (4). In the absence of maternal direction,

Mary is taught to read by the housekeeper and is instructed in French by the maid; for, her father, who "always exclaimed against female acquirements," is eager for her to remain ignorant (5). As the result of her emotional deprivation, Mary's "character early became singular and permanent. Her understanding was strong and clear, when not clouded by her feelings; but she was too much the creature of impulse and the slave of compassion" (7).

Like Mary, Mathilda also grows up without parental love: her mother dies (as Wollstonecraft did) soon after her child's birth, and her father, driven to despair at the loss of his wife, abandons his child, who is cared for until the age of sixteen by her aunt. Mathilda's aunt, who has "the coldest [heart] that ever filled a human breast" and who is "totally incapable of any affection," dismisses her nurse when the child is seven and prevents her from playing with the village girls (182). Thus Mathilda, like Mary, has a loveless childhood which she spends reading and observing nature. As the young Mary stays up at night "*conversing* with the Author of Nature, making verses, and singing hymns of her own composing" (11), the less religious Mathilda brings literary characters to life in her daydreams and forms "affections and intimacies with the aerial creations of [her] own brain" (185). Intelligent, unloved, and unsocialized, these young women are more prepared for death and the afterlife than for existence on earth.

Their emotionally deprived childhoods result, moreover, in their subsequent quests for father figures. Mary's "first favourites [are] men past the meridian of life, and of a philosophic turn," and she falls in love with an older man who urges her to "rely on him as if he was her father...the tenderest father could not more anxiously interest himself in the fate of a darling child, than he did in her's" (19, 35). Mathilda, on the other hand, develops an obsessional relationship with her own father, who returns after his sixteen-year absence: "I was always happy when near my father. It was a subject of regret to me whenever we were joined by a third person" (190). Neither relationship can be sustained: Mary cannot be the wife of her beloved Henry because she is already married, and Mathilda's relationship with her father comes to an end when he confesses his unnatural passion for her. The sickly Henry dies; Mathilda's father, unable to overcome his feelings for his daughter, commits suicide. Partly because of their emotionally deprived childhoods, characterized by obsessional fantasizing, neither Mary nor Mathilda can put these deaths into any kind of perspective: they live out their lives in despair, longing to rejoin their loved ones in death. At the end of *Mary,* the protagonist hopes to hasten "to that world *where there is neither marrying,* nor giving in marriage" (68), and Mathilda yearns to be reunited with her father "in an eternal mental union" (244).

In *A Vindication of the Rights of Women,* Wollstonecraft writes that "The parent who sedulously endeavours to form the heart and enlarge the understanding of his child, has given that dignity to the discharge of a duty, common to the whole animal world, that only reason can give" (153). At this crucially important task, the parents of Mary and Mathilda fail: they provide for their daughters' physical requirements, but never prepare them for life. Thus *Mary* and *Mathilda* are, among other things, indictments of parental neglect and insensitivity to the emotional developments of young women.

Although Shelley's *Valperga: or, the Life and Adventures of Castruccio, Prince of Lucca* (1823), set in fourteenth-century Italy, is ostensibly a political novel, it is also influenced by Wollstonecraft's educational principles: while the prophet Beatrice is an exemplar of the bad effects of the disorderly female education described in *Vindication* (unrestrained passion, the lack of a consistent purpose), Euthanasia has the clear moral vision of a woman whose education is based on rationality. Moreover, Euthanasia's rejection of Castruccio's proposal of marriage is strictly along lines set forth in Wollstonecraft's *Thoughts on the Education of Daughters,* in which Wollstonecraft recalls an exemplary woman

> ...warmly attached to an agreeable man, yet she saw his faults; his principles were unfixed, and his prodigal turn would have obliged her to have restrained every benevolent emotion of her heart. She exerted her influence to improve him, but in vain did she for years try to do it. Convinced of the impossibility, she determined not to marry him, though she was forced to encounter poverty and its attendants. (29)

Although Euthanasia has loved Castruccio, "the friend of her youth," he is the enemy of Florence and liberty, and he has seduced and then deserted Beatrice (II: 209). Thus she has no alternative but to suppress her feelings for him and break off their engagement:

> She considered Castruccio as bound to Beatrice;...She believed that he would be far happier in the passionate and unquestioning love of this enthusiast, than with her, who had lived too long to be satisfied alone with the affection of him she loved, but required in him a conformity of tastes to those she had herself cultivated, which in Castruccio was entirely wanting. (II: 194)

Euthanasia is clearly unlike many of the women of the later eighteenth century, who were, in Wollstonecraft's opinion, taught by society to be flighty coquettes and who allowed themselves to become "legally prostituted" in order to survive in a male-dominated world (*Vindication* 60). As in the case of the woman described in Wollstonecraft's anecdote, Euthanasia's rejection of her fiance causes her much unhappiness: he captures and destroys Valperga, her home, and ultimately banishes her. She dies unloved and is immediately forgotten. But she has remained true to her principles, and to the education her father gave her--this, to Wollstonecraft and Shelley, is a considerable achievement.

Shelley's exploration of female education is continued in one of the so-called conservative novels of her later period, *Lodore* (1835), in which all of the main female characters are shaped by their educations and in which two women, Ethel Villiers and Fanny Derham, are given uncommonly good educations by their doting fathers. In this novel, as in *Valperga,* Shelley emphasizes the importance of women receiving a masculine education rather than simply being taught accomplishments designed to prepare them for entry into society. Taken away from a traditional British upbringing to live with her father in the American wilderness, Ethel accompanies Lord Lodore on his excursions and is his devoted pupil: "There is a peculiarity in the education of a daughter, brought up by a father only, which tends to develop early a thousand of those portions of mind, which are folded up and often destroyed, under mere feminine tuition" (10). But although Ethel receives a sound moral training, her father fails to teach her self-reliance, which Shelley clearly sees as a deficiency: "A lofty sense of independence, is, in man, the best privilege of his nature. It cannot be doubted, but that it were for the happiness of the other sex that she were taught more to rely on and act for herself. But in the cultivation of this feeling, the education of [Lord Lodore] was lamentably deficient" (13). Thus, in the course of the novel, Ethel is able to withstand poverty and physical privation but depends solely on her financially inept husband to rescue them from penury. Her father prepares her to live in solitude in the wilds of Illinois, but in England she cannot exist apart from Edward Villiers, and Ethel's ignorance of money matters is yet another "faulty part of her father's system of education" (161).

In contrast, Fanny Derham's masculine education enables her to live independently and to pursue philosophical studies. Mrs. Greville describes Fanny's relationship to her valetudinarian father:

> She was his pupil--he her care...Fanny nursed her father, watched over
> his health and humours, with the tenderness and indulgence of a mother;

while he instructed her in the dead languages, and other sorts of abstruse learning, which seldom make a part of a girl's education. Fanny, to use her own singular language, loves philosophy, and pants after knowledge, and indulges in a thousand Platonic dreams. (58)

In her comparison of Ethel's and Fanny's educations, Shelley indicates that Fanny has been better prepared to survive life's vicissitudes:

Ethel had received, so to speak, a sexual education. Lord Lodore had formed his ideal of what a woman ought to be, of what he had wished to find his wife, and sought to mould his daughter accordingly. Mr. Derham...fashioned his offspring to be the wife of a frail human being, and instructed her to be yielding, and to make it her duty to devote herself to his happiness, and to obey his will. The other sought to guard his from all weakness, to make her complete in herself, and to render her independent and self-sufficing. (156)

Obviously a daughter who is trained to be self-reliant is better prepared to face life than is a woman who must depend on "a frail human being" to guide her, and Ethel's devotion to Villiers leads them both to debtors' prison, from which they are rescued by Ethel's estranged mother, Lady Lodore. Shelley also suggests that Fanny's education lends her a special moral strength:

Fanny zealously guarded her individuality, and would have scorned herself could she have been brought to place the treasures of her soul at the disposal of any power, except those moral laws which it was her earnest endeavour never to transgress. Religion, reason, and justice--these were the landmarks of her life. She was kind-hearted, generous, and true--so also was Ethel; but the one was guided by the tenderness of her heart, while the other consulted her understanding, and would have died rather than have acted contrary to its dictates. (156)

It is clear that Wollstonecraft, who believed that "virtue [arises] rather from the clear conviction of reason than the impulse of the heart" (*Vindication* 114), would have preferred Fanny's training in religion, reason, and justice to Ethel's "sexual education," which subordinates Ethel's morality to her husband's. And while Ethel is essentially passive, entrusting herself to providence and her husband's exertions, Fanny is active: she alerts Lady Lodore to Ethel's plight and thus paves the way for her friend's financial salvation. Here, again, Wollstonecraft would prefer Fanny's upbringing to Ethel's: as she writes in *Vindication,* "from their infancy women should either be shut up like eastern princes, or educated in such a manner as to be able to think and act for themselves" (47).

Although Fanny's classical education is in sharp contrast to Wollstonecraft's meager training at the Beverly day school, the character herself possesses Wollstonecraft-like independence and determination to fight against injustice. She expresses her social commitment in a rousing speech to Ethel in which she declares her impassioned advocacy on behalf of the "miserable and oppressed," when many are afraid to speak out or unable to (153). Shelley sometimes undercuts Fanny's idealism by revealing its otherworldly nature: this speech is succeeded by Fanny's declaration that "while [she] converse[s] each day with Plato, and Cicero, and Epictetus, the world...passes from before [her] like a vain shadow" (153). Still, clearly, Fanny's upbringing represents a valid alternative to Ethel's sexual education.

Despite the fact that Fanny is a relatively minor character in *Lodore,* her unconventionality makes her stand out; as Mellor notes, through her "Mary Shelley suggests that there might be an alternative identity and social role for women beyond those contained within the bourgeois family" (206). Shelley is, however, undecided about Fanny's fate. As an "anomaly little in accord with masculine taste" (153), she cannot be simply married off at the end of the book. After having sketched the fates of the other characters, Shelley ends *Lodore* with a tribute to Fanny's integrity and courage:

> In after times...the life of Fanny Derham [may] be presented as a useful lesson, at once to teach what goodness and genius can achieve in palliating the woes of life, and to encourage those, who would in any way imitate her, by an example of calumny refuted by patience, errors rectified by charity, and the passions of our nature purified and ennobled by an undeviating observance of those moral laws on which all human excellence is founded--a love of truth in ourselves, and a sincere sympathy with our fellow-creatures. (228)

Although Fanny Derham is an anomaly in her own time, after "a REVOLUTION in female manners" she could well provide an example for those "who would in any way imitate her" (*Vindication* 192). While *Lodore* focuses on the marital vicissitudes of Lady Lodore and Ethel Villiers, through Fanny Derham, Shelley hints at the possibility of another kind of life, in which a well-educated woman seeks fulfillment through philosophy and social activism rather than through marriage.

Thus Shelley is much closer to Wollstonecraft in her attitudes regarding the educational rights of women than many critics recognize.

And although Mellor argues that Shelley had a "continuing commitment to the [egalitarian] bourgeois family" (178), in my view Shelley's fiction suggests that well-educated women can exist independently of the family. While Euthanasia rejects her childhood sweetheart Castruccio and is thus able to continue her search for wisdom, "for ever enlarging her sphere of knowledge and feeling" (III: 195), Fanny Derham plans her life of social activism and academic pursuits entirely outside the domestic sphere. Moreover, even after having suffered years of widowhood, social ostracism, and ill-treatment by so-called political radicals, Shelley still remained committed to opposing the oppression of women. In October, 1838, she wrote in her journal: "If I have never written to vindicate the Rights of women, I have ever befriended women when oppressed--at every risk I have defended & supported victims to the social system" (II: 557). Although she was admittedly less outspoken then her mother, we do Shelley an injustice if we do not recognize that she too held feminist principles, one of the most important being the right of women to a proper education.

Works Cited

Mellor, Anne K. *Mary Shelley: Her Life, Her Fiction, Her Monsters.* New York: Routledge, 1988.

Norman, Sylva. "Mary Wollstonecraft Shelley (Life and Works)." In *Shelley and his Circle.* Ed. Kenneth Neill Cameron. Vol. III. Cambridge: Harvard University Press, 1970. 397-422.

Poovey, Mary. *The Proper Lady and the Woman Writer--Ideology as Style in the Works of Mary Wollstonecraft, Mary Shelley and Jane Austen.* Chicago: University of Chicago Press, 1984.

Shelley, Mary. *Frankenstein or, The Modern Prometheus. The Mary Shelley Reader.* Eds. Betty T. Bennett and Charles B. Robinson. New York: Oxford University Press, 1990.

___. *The Journals of Mary Shelley: 1814-1844.* Eds. Paula R. Feldman and Diana Scott-Kilvert. 2 Vols. Oxford: Clarendon Press, 1987.

___. *Lodore.* New York: Walls & Newell, 1835.

___. *Mathilda. The Mary Shelley Reader.* Eds. Betty T. Bennett and Charles E. Robinson. New York: Oxford University Press, 1990.

___. *The Fields of Fancy.* Ed. Elizabeth Nitchie. *Studies in Philology Extra Series #3.* Chapel Hill: University of North Carolina Press, 1959.

___. *Valperga: or, the Life and Adventures of Castruccio Prince of Lucca.* 3 Vols. London: G. and W.B. Whittaker, 1823.

Sunstein, Emily W. *Mary Shelley: Romance and Reality.* Baltimore: Johns Hopkins University Press, 1989.

Tayler, Irene, and Gina Luria. "Gender and Genre: Women in British Romantic

Literature." *What Manner of Woman. Essay on English and American Life and Literature.* Ed. Marlene Springer. New York: New York University Press, 1977.

Todd, Janet. "Frankenstein's Daughter: Mary Shelley and Mary Wollstonecraft," *Women and Literature* 4(1976): 18-27.

Tomalin, Claire. *The Life and Death of Mary Wollstonecraft.* Rev. ed. 1974; London: Penguin, 1992.

Wollstonecraft, Mary. *A Vindication of the Rights of Woman.* Ed. Carol H. Poston. 2nd ed. New York: Norton, 1988.

___. *Mary and the Wrongs of Woman.* Oxford: Oxford University Press, 1976.

___. *The Cave of Fancy. The Works of Mary Wollstonecraft.* Eds. Janet Todd and Marilyn Butler. 7 Vols. London: William Pickering. 1989. Vol. 1.

___. *Thoughts on the Education of Daughters. The Works of Mary Wollstonecraft.* Vol. 4.

Endnotes

[1] In her biography of Shelley, Sunstein argues that "She should be recognized as indeed her mother's daughter, heir to Wollstonecraft's Romantic feminism and to a fuller measure of punishment for it" (403). The case for Shelley's political conservatism was made by Sylva Norman, who writes: "[Shelley] could write sympathetically on the left-wing attitude, especially where Shelley, or a fictional Shelley-image, was in question; but, for herself, she lacked the inner fire. Too much in the other camp attracted her: social living, gentle manners, the advantages of culture" (409).

[2] Sunstein writes that "Godwin does not seem to have started Mary on Latin until she was an adolescent, and never taught her Greek, which was viewed as a male preserve and unnecessary for females, so that she looked up to those 'more cultivated' males who had read and written Greek and Latin since boyhood" (41).

The Alienation of Family in Mary Shelley's *Frankenstein*

Karla Alwes

> With us the susceptible imagination of the mother seems to express itself only in monsters.
>
> --Winckelman[1]

Born in 1797, Mary Wollstonecraft Godwin lived until the age of 16 with her father, stepmother, and step siblings. Her letters reveal that she felt herself living the same alienation within her own family that, as the writer Mary Shelley, she would impose on her fictive families in *Frankenstein* in 1818.

Shelley's life began with the death of her mother. Ten days after giving birth, Mary Wollstonecraft died from "childbed sickness" (Tropp 11), so that the daughter would eventually come to know her mother only through reading Wollstonecraft's works, which Shelley did extensively. Moreover, all knowledge of anything maternal in Shelley's own life came from reading rather than from actual experience, for Shelley could find no familial comfort in her father's second wife, Mary Jane Clairmont, whom Shelley describes in her journal as "a woman I shudder to think of" (23 1 November 1814).

Martin Tropp writes that Shelley's "fondest childhood memories," precipitated by the lack of love toward her stepmother and the "half-obsessive" love she felt for her father, were of "solitary pastimes" (12).[2] In the 1831 introduction to *Frankenstein* Shelley discusses the solitary pleasures of her childhood:

> It is not singular that, as the daughter of two persons of distinguished literary celebrity, I should very early in life have thought of writing...my favourite pastime, during the hours given me for recreation, was to "write stories." Still I had a dearer pleasure than this, which was the formation

> of castles in the air--the indulging in waking dreams--the following up
> trains of thought, which had for their subject the formation of a
> succession of imaginary incidents.   My dreams were at once more
> fantastic and agreeable than my writing....I accounted for them to
> nobody; they were my refuge when annoyed--my dearest pleasure when
> free. (167)

It is clear that Shelley recognizes the debt to her own literary family
early in life. Lineage would become problematic in *Frankenstein,*
however, and the "waking dreams" of Shelley's childhood imagination
lead to the nightmare that she experiences the night *Frankenstein* was
conceived:

> My imagination, unbidden, possessed and guided me, gifting the
> successive images that arose in my mind with a vividness far beyond the
> usual bounds of reverie....I saw the hideous phantasm of a man stretched
> out, and then,...stir with an uneasy, half vital motion. Frightful it must
> be; for supremely frightful would be the effect of any human endeavour
> to mock the stupendous mechanism of the Creator of the world. (170)

"I opened [my eyes] in terror," Shelley recalls following the nightmare
(170). It would be a frightening tale that attempts to "mock the
stupendous mechanism of the Creator of the World." As such, it also
subverts the creative principle of the maternal and would illuminate and
develop the theme of the isolation of life-in-death, life bereft of the
maternal, similar to that of Coleridge's own nightmarish *Ancient
Mariner,* a poem Shelley had read, possibly more than once, during the
year she wrote *Frankenstein.*[3] "I bid my hideous progeny go forth and
prosper," Shelley instructs both monster and tale (171), and the only
instance of successful lineage evoked in the tale itself is that between
author and creation, regardless of the "hideous" state of the progeny.
There is no lineage in the novel because all aspects of the maternal are
either aborted or subverted to the masculine. Sandra M. Gilbert and
Susan Gubar write:

> [Frankenstein's] "pregnancy" and childbirth are obviously manifested by
> the existence of the paradoxically huge being who emerges from his
> "workshop of filthy creation," but even the descriptive language of his
> creation myth is suggestive: "incredible labours," "emaciated with
> confinement,"...and in his isolated workshop of filthy creation--filthy
> because obscenely sexual--he collects and arranges materials furnished
> by "the dissecting room and the slaughterhouse." (232-33)

Victor Frankenstein can provide no heir to his life, despite his act of creating the monster, because the act is one of degeneration rather than regeneration, pursued through the solipsism of masculine science rather than via the procreative feminine. "The dissecting room and the slaughterhouse," whence come his materials, invert life into death. "After the [m]onster's birth,"...Frankenstein is a disintegrated being--an embodiment of emotion and also of imagination minus intellect" (Spark 165). The monster's creation is an inversion of the process of birth, whereby the creator becomes "disintegrated" rather than made psychically whole, fragmented from others rather than embraced into community, and the creator dissolves into his creation. The "family" that is predecessor to the monster will be summarily destroyed because of Victor's alienation from them and from himself following the "birth" of his creation. With the death of every major character in the novel, including Victor himself, all familial relationships are destroyed, leaving Captain Walton, the tale's primary narrator, who frames the story in his letters to his sister, in the same solitary state at the end that he condemned at the beginning. In a lament similar to the monster's later plea to Victor to create a mate for him, Walton tells his sister: "I have no friend, Margaret:"

> when I am glowing with the enthusiasm of success, there will be none to participate [in] my joy; if I am assailed by disappointment, no one will endeavour to sustain me in dejection.(18)

Written in epistolary form, the novel offers no real community between narrators, as each parlays his individual story into the larger story that subsumes them and that becomes ultimately the letters of Captain Walton to his sister, Mrs. Saville. In an early letter to the bodiless, voiceless Mrs. Saville (who exists outside the narration) Walton expresses the alienation that is found in the absence of direct community:

> I shall commit my thoughts to paper...but that is a poor medium for the communication of feeling. I desire the company of a man who could sympathize with me; whose eyes would reply to mine. You may deem me romantic, my dear sister, but I bitterly feel the want of a friend. (18)

Accordingly, the loss of family within Victor Frankenstein's narration is set within Walton's own apparently close relationship with his sister; his similar fears of being alone, of being cut off from her, his childlike "want of a friend," further illuminate the creator Frankenstein's own loss of family. The epistolary narration enforces all knowledge of the creator and his creation to be gained by Mrs. Saville passively and intellectually rather than empirically, just as Shelley's knowledge of her mother had been gained through reading her words rather than hearing them. Maternal closeness is absent from the story altogether.

Walton tells his sister that he is "going to unexplored regions, to 'the land of mist and snow;' but I shall kill no albatross, therefore do not be alarmed for my safety" (19). The obvious reference to Coleridge's *Ancient Mariner* reinforces Walton's own solitariness, as the Ancient Mariner is product and prototype of Romantic alienation and, further, of loss of salvation, a theme pertinent to *Frankenstein*. Whether enforced or invited, solitude is the only reality in the novel, and with the concurrent loss of each character who tries and fails to find community within family, solitude becomes akin to solipsism.

Marriage, a metaphor frequently invoked by Romantic writers to represent unity, is repressed into a disastrous fallacy in *Frankenstein*. Victor's father Alphonse finds his future bride Caroline Beaufort kneeling at her dead father's coffin, "weeping bitterly":

> He came like a protecting spirit to the poor girl, who committed herself to his care, and after the interment of his friend he conducted her to Geneva, and placed her under the protection of a relation. Two years after this event Caroline became his wife. (27)

As it is the death of her father that brings the two of them together, the child bride is more like an orphan charged to Alphonse Frankenstein's care than a fitting wife. Elizabeth Lavenza, Victor's cousin who becomes his bride, also arrives within the Frankenstein family following a death--that of her mother, with a charge from her father that Alphonse "should consider her as [his] own daughter....Reflect upon this proposition; and decide whether you would prefer educating your niece yourself or being brought up by a stepmother" (27). Both Caroline and Elizabeth become members of the Frankenstein family because of the ends of their own families--losing father and mother, respectively--and both become the only hope for community to the Frankenstein men. Although Caroline will live long enough to give birth to the doomed Frankenstein children, Elizabeth's marriage to Victor is the cause of her own death. Just as Shelley achieves "hideous progeny" with the monster's creation, so is there an even more hideous lack of progeny within the novel itself. Life and lineage are consistently thwarted because families are splintered into solipsistic and alienated individuals who have neither social nor emotional intercourse.

Chris Baldick writes that the "creation of the monster is an attempt to create life without encountering female sexuality" (49). As many critics have noted, Victor is afraid of both Elizabeth's sexuality and her desire to be close to him, a fear that masquerades only partially as a fear for Elizabeth's safety on their wedding night. But all attempts at safety and emotional sustenance for the female traditionally offered by the male during courtship and marriage are starkly parodied in the novel when Elizabeth dies on her wedding night, alone on the nuptial bed, left by Victor who unsuccessfully and distantly (both physically and emotionally) attempts to protect her (and himself) from the monster. As is so often the case in the novel, this attempt at community, a conventional rite of passage to signify the end of individual solitude, fails disastrously, with Elizabeth becoming a corpse on her wedding night, "an 'exchange' for the transformation of a corpse [the monster] into a living being" (Baldick 49). The spiritual and sexual union meant to occur during nuptial rites becomes instead the morbid and grotesque union of dead Elizabeth and the monster who killed her. More specifically, the dead Elizabeth becomes symbolically "united," through death, with the monster's own dead female mate whom Victor has created then destroyed. Victor is left alive once again (like the Ancient Mariner, he survives all deaths in the novel, until his own, in order to tell the tale), alienated and impotent outside the growing circle of the accumulating dead.

Johanna Smith suggests that Victor's creation and destruction of the female monster is a "parody of [the] women's fates [in the novel]. Elizabeth's creation and murder show that women function not in their own right but rather as signals of and conduits for men's relations with other men" (283). At the novel's end all the Frankenstein women--splintered into mother, wife, and daughter--are dead, victims of either the masculine predilection for absolute knowledge through science or, as in Caroline's case, victim of the feminine cultural rite of self-sacrifice (her death is precipitated by nursing the scarlet-fever-stricken Elizabeth). The only women left alive survive outside the Frankenstein family circle and outside the reality of the story as well--Safie, the Arabian who is postulated as the ideal lover in the monster's tale (within his framed narrative), and Mrs. Saville, the ideal sister who exists outside the tale altogether.

Bodiless and voiceless, Mrs. Saville serves only as the narrator Walton's passive listener. Although Victor's narration begins with two sister figures--Elizabeth and Justine--Mrs. Saville is the only remaining sister, whose survival depends on Walton's narrative. Mrs. Saville's status outside the family places her outside all action within the tale--impervious to the masculine contrivances that are masked within the novel as "heroic ambitions" (Baldick 187), but she is also the first "dead" woman in the tale. We never see, hear, or intuit her presence except for Walton's letters to her, yet it is because of her role as recipient of the letters that the story endures.

Mrs. Saville's lack of physicality and voice, which could be deemed Mary Shelleyan androgyny, enables her survival, but Smith notes that "no women in the novel speak directly: everything we hear from and about them is filtered through the three masculine narrators" (270). That the women's lives and voices are created for them by Victor, Captain Walton, or the monster signifies their collective doom, just as the monster's doom is ordained for him by Victor, certainly the most androcentric, and thus solitary, of the male narrators.

Outside all action, Mrs. Saville is never in danger and never in doubt of her survival because she is given no voice with which to articulate either. Her brother frequently voices doubts over his own survival to her, however, but such doubts exist only prior to meeting Victor Frankenstein and hearing the tale of survival that is contingent on the solipsistic masculine pursuits through empirical science. Walton's final expression of doubt, uttered just before he finds Victor "nearly frozen, and his body dreadfully emaciated by fatigue and suffering," asks his sister to "remember me with affection, should you never hear from me again" (22, 20). Upon hearing and relating Victor's tale, Walton, like the wedding guest who hears the recital of the Ancient Mariner and thus becomes a sadder yet wiser man, recognizes his own survival to be contingent on suffering through knowledge.

Walton's doubts over his survival prefigure the novel's theme: it is a fight for survival with masculine knowledge pitted against a feminized sense of community, and the women involved in the struggle are already dead when Victor's narrative to Walton begins. The monster, who initially yearns for community rather than knowledge, speaks directly to the horrors of acquiring the latter: "…sorrow only increased with knowledge. Oh, that I had for ever remained in my native wood, nor known or felt beyond the sensations of hunger, thirst, and heat!" (89). The monster's initiation from child to adult is defined by the solitary acquisition of knowledge: "Of what a strange nature is knowledge! It clings to the mind, when it has once seized on it, like a lichen on the rock. I wished sometimes to shake off all thought and feeling; but I learned that there was but one means to overcome the sensation of pain, and that was death--a state which I feared yet did not understand" (89). To become masculine in the novel is to abandon the feminine through knowledge that "clings to the mind," letting go only at death.

More specifically, Muriel Spark comments that it is the

> emotional and the intellectual that conflict in the form of Frankenstein and his [m]onster. The culminating emotional frustration by the intellect is reached in the murder of Frankenstein's bride by the [m]onster. Thereafter, Frankenstein's hysterical pursuit of his fleeting reason completes the story of his madness--a condition perceived in the tale only by the Genevan magistrate, who... "endeavoured" says Frankenstein, "to soothe me as a nurse does a child." (165)

Victor's "fleeting reason" precipitates and culminates in his overt madness. When his intellect is gone, his emotional/feminized self is all that remains, and he is thus treated "as a child" by a stranger who recognized the vulnerability that is caused by Victor's loss of masculinity.[4]

Throughout the tale, Victor attempts to displace the feminized aspect of himself, and thus assure masculine survival, by transferring all emotional qualities onto his own created persona of Elizabeth--ideal sister, woman, wife:

> She was docile and good tempered, yet gay and playful as a summer insect. Although she was lively and animated, her feelings were strong and deep, and her disposition uncommonly affectionate...she appeared the most fragile creature in the world. While I admired her understanding and fancy, I loved to tend on her, as I should on a favourite animal. (28)

Victor's perception of Elizabeth, seen through the eyes of patriarchal narrative, reduces her "affection," crucial to the creation of community, to that of an ephemeral "summer insect" or a "favourite animal" on whom he dotes. Victor's description, that is, creates Elizabeth, a corpse at the outset, as a living prototype of the feminine in order to attempt to regain the masculine sensibility lost to the madness of scientific failure. His creation of the monster, too, like his creation of Elizabeth's feminine self, allows Victor full masculine dominance, as the act of parthenogenetic creation usurps "not the privilege of God but the reproductive power of women" (Baldick 51).

Listening to the tale, Walton's psychical journey into the mind of Victor Frankenstein becomes, like his own literal journey, one of initiation into the masculine:

Walton's abortive trip to the North Pole is clearly a classic journey of initiation....Learning from Frankenstein's failure, and passing the trial of the [m]onster's nearly persuasive arguments, Walton chooses the path that will lead back to society, having gained new awareness of himself and new knowledge for his culture. (Tropp 8-9)

The "culture" to which Walton returns is strictly defined within the novel as that of masculine prerogative, and, with Victor as prototype, Walton's fears over his survival are aborted along with his expedition to the North Pole. At the novel's end, Walton relates to his sister that the monster "sprung from the cabin-window...upon the ice-raft which lay close to the vessel. He was soon borne away by the waves, and lost in darkness and distance" (165). The "darkness and distance" that now lie between the monster and Walton effectively manifest Walton's newfound lack of desire for community and dismissal of the desire for masculine knowledge, characterized by solitude, that returns Walton to the aforementioned culture. Throughout the narrative between the monster and himself, concluding in an admonition of the monster by Walton, it is clear that Walton's sympathies lie with Victor Frankenstein--the solitary creator, usurper, and scientist--rather than with his creation, who desires above all community with others and abjures his self-taught knowledge. A lack of community is enforced upon rather than chosen by women in the novel. And Walton, who openly reveres Victor, becomes Victor's third and only successful creation because his narration of Victor's story, as well as his turning of deaf ears to the monster's plea for compassion, keeps the solitary masculine icon alive. As Tropp says, Walton has learned from Frankenstein's failure, and such knowledge leads him back to the very culture that Victor Frankenstein abandoned (9).

William Veeder notes that, in order to further the patriarchal culture, Victor "molds from clay a being more suitable to his purposes than mortal Elizabeth can ever be" (111). In the culture that Victor first attempts to sustain through dominance, but eventually spurns, Elizabeth exists as the other--secondary in Victor's mind even to the monster himself. "Behind this male desire to mold," Veeder continues, "is a will to power which Mary Shelley exposes throughout her fiction," and the novel "insists that the humble but crucial molding which counts most, the cultivation of a human relationship, can only be deformed if subjected to the random violence of will" (111-12). The frightening specter of feminine community, as recounted in Victor's narration of his nightmare to Walton, denies the solipsistic power of the alienated male and transfers all power to the female, as the nightmare vision of bride Elizabeth becomes the dead mother of Caroline and finally the monster himself, created in Victor's dream by the female rather than the male:

> I thought I saw Elizabeth, in the bloom of health, walking in the streets of Ingolstadt...as I imprinted the first kiss on her lips, they became livid with the hue of death; her features appeared to change, and I thought that I held the corpse of my dead mother in my arms, a shroud enveloped her form, and I saw the grave-worms crawling in the folds of the flannel. I started from my sleep with horror...I beheld the wretch--the miserable monster whom I had created. (43)

The "motherless birth" (Johnson 9) of the monster is avenged in this dream of transferred identities between Elizabeth and Caroline, who compose the only legitimate avenue to both human relationships and procreation, now dead and dismissed by Victor's illegitimate usurpation.

The death of the maternal in the novel leaves all the characters, including Walton and the monster, orphans.[5] There is no possibility of progeny because of the loss of desire for human community. Despite Walton's newfound affection for "culture," the narrative ends in as solitary a fashion as the vessel's journey itself, with the unregenerative "darkness and distance" as the Captain's only companions (165).

Virginia Woolf writes: "we think back through our mothers if we are women" (qtd. in Gilbert and Gubar 243). But history has eluded our mothers as well as our daughters. Women, like the monster himself, are characterized by the "unique knowledge of what it is like to be born free of history," with no past, no collective self knowledge from which to draw succor (Gilbert and Gubar 238 [Rieger xxx]). Victor and Walton, conversely, have *only* the past. The Arctic region that Walton traverses and in which he hears the tale of Victor and his monster allows no growth, no life--the nature that, like the female, should be fecund, is instead barren and solitary, relegated to the past, and as moribund as the masculine knowledge that is evoked within it. All procreation in *Frankenstein* becomes merely recreation, imitative of life. And the knowledge derived from it, orphaned and alienated from the true creative process that is female, destroys all who seek to share it.

Works Cited

Baldick Chris. *In Frankenstein's Shadow. Myth, Monstrosity, and Nineteenth-Century Writing.* Oxford: Clarendon Press, 1987.

Gilbert Sandra M. and Susan Gubar. *The Madwoman in the Attic. The Woman Writer and the Nineteenth-Century Imagination.* New Haven: Yale University Press, 1979.

Johnson, Barbara. "My Monster/My Self." *Diacritics* 12(1982): 2-10.

Jones, Frederick L., ed. *Mary Shelley's Journal.* Norman: University of Oklahoma Press, 1947.

Nitchie, Elizabeth. *Mary Shelley. Author of Frankenstein.* New Brunswick: Rutgers University Press, 1953; rpt Westport: Greenwood, 1970.

Rieger, James. "Introduction." *Frankenstein (the 1818 text).* Indianapolis: Bobbs-Merrill, 1974.

Senf, Carol A. "Mary Shelley." *Encylopedia of Romanticism, Culture in Britain, 1780s-1830s.* Ed. Laura Dabundo. New York: Garland, 1992.

Shelley, Mary. *Frankenstein, or, The Modern Prometheus. The Mary Shelley Reader.* Eds. Betty T. Bennett and Charles E. Robinson. New York: Oxford University Press, 1990. 13-171.

Smith, Johanna M. "Cooped Up: Feminine Domesticity in *Frankenstein*." *Case Studies in Contemporary Criticism.* Ed. Johanna M. Smith. Boston: Bedford, 1992. 270-85.

Spark, Muriel. *Mary Shelley.* New York: Dutton, 1987.

Tropp, Martin. *Mary Shelley's Monster.* Boston: Houghton, 1976.

Veeder, William. *Mary Shelley and Frankenstein: The Fate of Androgny.* Chicago: University of Chicago Press, 1986.

Endnotes

[1] Quoted in Veeder (105). Such a quote is appropriate to Shelley's own fictional loss of the maternal. The absence of the mother from the family is a form of abandonment made "monstrous" in the patriarchal culture.

[2] Nitchie cites an unpublished letter by Mary Shelley regarding her father William Godwin: "Until I met Shelley I [could] justly say he was my God--and I remember many childish instances of the [ex]cess of attachment I bore for Him" (89). Senf writes that because of her father's influence on her early childhood, Shelley's "fiction often features daughters who admire their fathers" (523).

[3] In her journal Shelley frequently notes that Percy Bysshe also read Coleridge's *Ancient Mariner* aloud. During 1816, she read Byron's *Childe Harold, Canto III* as well, a likely analogue to the grandeurs of the natural and cultural wilderness depicted in *Frankenstein*.

[4] Captain Walton frequently, but favorably, compares himself to a child, especially when he seeks the relationship and companionship of a sibling. He writes to his sister: "I shall satiate my ardent curiosity with the sight of a part of the world never before visited, and may tread a land never before imprinted by the foot of man. These are my enticements, and they are sufficient to conquer all fear of danger or death, and to induce me to commence this laborious voyage with the joy a child feels when he embarks in a little boat, with his holiday mates, on an expedition of discovery up his native river" (15, 16). Of Victor Frankenstein, Walton says, "I begin to love him as a brother" (23). It is his puerile fantasy, to be a part of a family and yet independent of others, that precipitates Walton's excitement over both his journey and his newfound friend.

[5] Gilbert and Gubar note that Shelley was fascinated with "the disastrous tale of the child who becomes 'an orphan and a beggar,'" and she uses this phrase twice in the novel to describe Elizabeth Lavenza. Gilbert and Gubar state that "the early alienation from the patriarchal chain-of-being signalled by their [Caroline and Elizabeth's] orphanhood prefigures the hellish fate in store for them and their family" (227).

Mary Shelley, Shakespeare, and the Romantic Theatre

Vincent F. Petronella

Mary Shelley's novels are prose romances pulsating with a vitality drawn from a wide spectrum of dramatic literature that inevitably includes Shakespeare but that also involves different attempts at a staged drama in the Romantic era. I wish to consider in her work features derived not only from Shakespeare but also from the transformed--sometimes transmogrified-Shakespeare found in the Romantic drama. Specifically, my focus of attention springs from three such features (the self, graveyard settings, and tempests) and the connections among them. Variations on these are exceedingly instructive in regard to exploring Shelley's dramatic ability, especially since the relationship between the dramatic heritage of Shakespeare and the Romantic theatre has been traditionally strong and productive.

Before meeting Percy Shelley, Mary Godwin enjoyed a bookish existence. Her informal schooling and casual reading included Shakespeare and many other dramatists of the classical and early modern periods. Later her education developed through her relationship with Percy Shelley. Between 1815 and the summer of 1816 (i.e., eighteen months before starting *Frankenstein*) Mary Shelley read "some ninety works that are representative of her permanent interests" (Sunstein 106). Although her reading included Goethe, Schiller, Caldern, Dante, Tasso, Ariosto, and Alfieri, her central dramatic readings at this time were in the works of prominent English authors such as Shakespeare, Milton, the dramas of Coleridge and Byron, the dramas of Matthew "Monk" Lewis, and Joanna Baillie's Romantic plays.

Mary Shelley was closely involved with work on *The Cenci* (1819). In 1818, Percy found in Livorno the manuscript called in English the "Relation of the Death of the Family of the Cenci." Mary may have translated it from the Italian that very year. Contemplating the history of Beatrice Cenci and her doomed family, Percy Shelley encouraged Mary Shelley to write a dramatic version of the fuliginous details recorded in the "Relation" and also continually urged her to translate Vittorio Alfieri's *Mirra* (1795), a romantic drama centering on the Ovidian story of an incestuous relationship between father and daughter. Confident in Mary's ability, Percy believed that she possessed the dramatic talent to transform the grim facts of the prose narrative into an effective stage play.

When the Leigh and Marianne Hunt family joined the Shelley household, the little circle became active in theatregoing. Sunstein says that because Hunt played the piano and sang very well, he inspired in Mary an increased love of music and a new interest in still another theatrical form, the opera, especially Mozart's, which she preferred above all the other operas the rest of her life (134). As an avid playgoer, Hunt gladly accompanied Mary to theatres "so that Mary's girlhood excitement for theatre revived" (Sunstein 134). Shelley himself was not attracted to the theatre (Otten 14-15), no doubt because of his disappointment with the quality of the staging and the acting. Nevertheless, in May of 1817 (in Mary's sixth month of pregnancy) Percy and Mary went to stage performances in London, where she was dazzled by the magnificent acting of Edmund Kean (Sunstein 135).

Frankenstein, finished at Marlow May 14, 1817, convinced Percy Shelley that she had a dramatic gift. He encouraged her to write a play. But wishing first to prepare herself thoroughly, she began, Sunstein explains, a systematic two-year course of reading essays on drama in addition to the great English, French, Latin, and Italian playwrights (138) with Shakespeare at the core of her studies. Underscoring this immersion in Shakespeare was Hunt's habit of calling Mary "Marina" after Shakespeare's peerless heroine in *Pericles*--she who was "Born in a tempest, when [her] mother died" (IV.i.18) and who had difficulties with a stepmother. Before leaving for Italy, Mary and Percy spent most of February and part of March of 1818, socializing in London and from the best box seats taking their fill of the opera and theatre (Sunstein 147). During their London stay, Gothic plays like William Dimond's *Bride of Abydos* played at Drury Lane and elsewhere (Evans 244).

From England they headed to Italy, eventually Milan, where a teacher was engaged with whom Mary studied Italian literature (Sunstein 152).

Her reading at this time is relevant to her development as a drama-conscious novelist in that it included the work of three influential playwrights: Pietro Metastasio (1698-1782) and Carlo Gozzi (1720-1806), who were associated with early Romantic drama on the Continent, and Vincenzo Monti (1754-1828), a later Romantic dramatist who was a contemporary of the Shelleys.

Metastasio wrote his dramatic pieces in either blank verse (what the Italians call *verso sciolto*) or a verse with loosely structured rhyme. He consciously derives one of his key themes from Pierre Corneille: Love in opposition to duty, a central dramatic tension that occurs often in Shelley's novels. Gozzi advocates full theatrical exploitation of fantasy and imagination and hence wrote dramas in opposition to the bourgeois realism of Carlo Goldoni (1707-1793). For example, Gozzi's dramatic fable of *The Blue Monster* (*Il mostro turchino*) is something of a comical version of reactions to monstrosities. It is a *Frankenstein* with laughs. Monti was capable of a Shakespearean style and uses blank verse not only in his dramas but also in shorter poetic works like *Prometheus,* his celebration of Napoleonic successes. So in the Italian playwrights, Shelley found various stylistic and thematic details that would give dramatic force to her prose fiction.

Frankenstein, which would be fashioned by Richard Brinsely Peake into a stage drama in 1823, has itself the sweep not only of a Romantic novel but also of a Romantic drama. Framed by the sea-voyage of Captain Robert Walton, the work consciously echoes Coleridge's *Rime of the Ancient Mariner* as it suggests the comings and going of sea-voyaging characters in plays such as *Othello, Pericles,* and *The Tempest.* Hamlet, who is for a time out at sea with pirates and who undergoes his particular sea change, also comes to mind here. What is more, like a Hamlet writ large, Victor Frankenstein is haunted by that which he needs to do but, unlike Hamlet, never succeeds in accomplishing. If Victor has a literal monster manifesting misdirected intelligence and power, Hamlet has the intelligent, powerful, yet monstrous Claudius with whom to contend. And the contention in either case results in an anguished self, a protagonist who turns dangerously inward as he tries desperately to maintain a link to others: Victor's Ophelia is Elizabeth Lavenza (and in some ways, Justine Moritz); his Horatio is Henry Clerval.

Jeffrey Cox tells us that many of the figures in Gothic and Romantic drama "owe a debt to Hamlet and his self-reflective doubt" (64), but we also see it in Gothic and Romantic novels (like *Frankenstein*). When Peake dramatized Shelley's novel as *Presumption; or The Fate of*

Frankenstein in 1823, the stage production of which Shelley herself saw and enjoyed despite the liberties taken with the text, Peake has Victor uttering a life-death soliloquy toward the close of the first scene, about the point at which Hamlet utters his first soliloquy (II.ii). Following the characterization and the soliloquizing of Shelley's *Frankenstein,* Peake's adaptation has him say:

> To examine the causes of life--I have had recourse to death--I have Seen how the fine form of man has been wasted and degraded--have beheld the corruption of death succeed to the blooming cheek of life! (139)

The lines are almost verbatim from Shelley and capture something of the rhythmical cadence in her work that very often reads as blank verse. What follows is the relevant passage from her novel, transcribed poetically:

> To examine the causes of life,
> we must first have recourse to death.
> I became acquainted with the science
> of anatomy: but this was not sufficient.
> I must also observe the natural decay
> and corruption of the human body....
> I beheld the corruption of death succeed
> to the blooming cheek of life, until
> from the midst of this darkness
> a sudden light broke in upon me. (53)

Victor's lines come from a context referring to the charnel house and the vaults of the churchyard, but it is near the close of *Frankenstein* that we find the returned protagonist--as is the case of the returned Hamlet-- in the churchyard contemplating mortality as he has never quite done before:

> As night approached, I found myself at the entrance of the cemetery where William, Elizabeth, and my father reposed. I entered it, and approached the tomb which marked their graves....I call on you, spirits of the dead; and on you wandering ministers of vengeance, to aid and conduct me in my work. Let the cursed and hellish monster drink deep of agony; let him feel the despair that now torments me. (168-69)

Victor's soliloquizing here recalls Hamlet the Revenger and even echoes one of the Prince's lines to Horatio: "Well teach you to drink [deep] ere you depart" (I.ii.175). The tragedy of Victor Frankenstein, like that of Hamlet, will find many persons, despite their degree of guilt or innocence, drinking deeply of agony before all concludes catastrophically. Has the pain, the death, and the mental fracturing resulted from a protagonist who has slowly lost his mind? The question often asked of Hamlet is one to ask of Frankenstein. Early in the novel, Victor says to Captain Walton, "Remember, I am not recording the vision of a madman" (54), wishing to assure his listener that his mind is intact despite recent tempestuous events.

The storm of life, as it is linked with literal storms and the storminess within the anguished mind, is a powerful Shakespearean motif that spills into all genres of Romantic literature, an almost obligatory ingredient in the Gothic novel as well as the Gothic drama. The so-called haunted summer of 1816 on Geneva's Lake Léman with its cast of bright luminaries (both Shelleys, Byron, Polidori, Clare Clairmont, and even Monk Lewis) was helped along by the tempestuous behavior of nature. Both the 1817 preface and the 1831 introduction to *Frankenstein* mention the inclement weather that forced the inmates of Maison Chapuis (the Shelleys' residence) to gather at Byron's Villa Diodati. There they remained indoors and looked inward, in each case addressing the self through responding to ghost stories and attempting to create similar ones. *Manfred,* Byron's Romantic drama published in the year of *Frankenstein* (1817), shows a hero, Prometheus-like, who provokes elemental conflict. Similarly, Shelley's modern Prometheus contends with the elements. Victor makes his way into the valley and then into the village of Chamounix observing the drama of the sublime unfolding before him near the peak of Mont Blanc: "The sight of the awful and majestic/in nature, had indeed always the effect/of solemnising my mind and causing/me to forget the passing cares of life" (88; line breaks added). With these quasi-blank-verse lines Victor connects sublime awfulness with the self. Like King Lear and Prospero, Romantic heroes assert individual selfhood, reveal inward turmoil, and offer a cosmic perspective as they address the tempest as another character in the drama. All of them enact what is described by Brutus just after an ominous storm strikes Rome in Shakespeare's *Julius Caesar:* the upsetting of "the state of man," which "Like to a little kingdom, suffers...The nature of an insurrection" (II.i.67-69), Victor Frankenstein speaks similarly: "I closed my eyes that night [after hearing Professor Waldman's inspiring lecture]. My internal being was in a state of insurrection and turmoil" (51). In *Frankenstein,* Victor has already told Walton of a storm that possesses such force as to utterly destroy an oak tree (45-46). More tempests, literal and figurative, follow the careers of both Brutus and Frankenstein.

By contrast, *Valperga; or, The Life of Castruccio, Prince of Lucca* (1823) is a political novel. But like Frankenstein, it portrays a self-centered protagonist and his woman. Each has lurking within both the Macbeth and the Lady Macbeth principles (Blumberg 92). Shelley also incorporates details from neo-Shakespearean Romantic dramas like *The Cenci*. In *Valperga,* the prophetess Beatrice, who eventually becomes Castruccio's love interest, is likened to the viciously abused daughter of the debased Roman count:

> Her deep black eyes, half concealed by their heavy lids, her curved lips, and face formed in a perfect oval the rising colour that glowed in her cheeks which, though her complexion was pure and delicate, were tinged by the suns of Italy, formed a picture such as Guido has since imagined, when he painted a Virgin or an Ariadne, or which he copied from the life when he painted the unfortunate Beatrice Cenci. (II: 17-18)

The novel surpasses descriptive allusion when it actually shows the Prince of Lucca at the court of the English King Edward II where the favorite Gaveston causes a stir. Shelley knew Marlowe's play on the subject and tuned into Marlovian blank verse. In the second volume of *Valperga,* Shelley tells of the heroine Countess Euthanasia dei Adimari's return to Valperga, her castle built upon a lofty rocky perch near the Tuscan city of Lucca. Her return and subsequent reunion with the Prince Castruccio of Lucca are marked by the onset of an autumnal tempest:

> The thunder broke in tremendous and continued peals, and the rain awoke in a moment the dried up sources of the mountain torrents; yet their liquid career was not heard amidst the tumult; for if the thunder paused, the echoes prolonged the sound; and all nature seemed labouring with the commotion. (II: 139-40)

The full value of appropriate vowel tones (especially the open "o's") combines with enough sibilants to give poetic coloring to the passage. Again the rhythm--although not the methodical blank verse of Mary Shelley's two poetic Ovidian dramas, *Proserpine* and *Midas* (1820)--resembles the line heard in many Romantic dramas.

It is heard, for example, in Coleridge's *Remorse* (1813), a recast of his *Osorio* (completed in 1797, the year of Shelley's birth). Some years later Coleridge was in Skinner Street to pay the Godwins a visit, during which, it is said, Mary and Jane hid behind a sofa to hear him read *The*

Rime of the Ancient Mariner. Whether Shelley read either *Osorio* or *Remorse* is not known; her work, however, shows that this kind of dramatic writing appealed to her. In Act 1, Don Alvar tells Dona Teresa,

> On a rude rock,
> A rock, methought, fast by a grove of firs,
> Whose thready leaves to the low-breathing gale
> Made a soft sound most like the distant ocean.
> ... and ere the midnight hour
> A storm came on, mingling all sounds of fear,
> That woods, and sky, and mountains, seemed one havock
> The second flash of lightning shewed a tree
> Hard by me, newly scathed. (I.ii.294-97; 302-306)

Tempests corresponding to the self become a stock in trade in the Romantic drama, and Shelley's novels reflect this by use of the tempestuous details themselves cast in rhythmical prose and lyrical diction that contribute to thematic and character development.

Euthanasia's reunion with Castruccio in *Valperga* is played out, Blumberg explains, "beneath a magnificent thunderstorm, an element of the sublime that [Shelley] often employed to underscore crisis, moments of discovery...and moments of intense emotion" (85). That Euthanasia and Castruccio mutually reject one another as lovers results in nature's sublime disapproval. This suggests the medieval, and hence hierarchically ordered, microcosm-macrocosmic correspondences that are fitting for the trecento setting of the novel. At the same time, the activity of the sublime in nature is always of interest to the Romantic who uses it to explore the relationships between inner and outer worlds. Tempests, whether literally presented onstage, verbally and figuratively imagined, or mixed, effectively provide a theatrical context and accompaniment for the collapse of human relationships, of social or domestic connections.

Shelley apparently knew the dramatic work of Joanna Baillie (1762-1851), whose long life rendered her a contemporary. She may have been aware of Baillie's plays in either England, where they were performed, or in Scotland, which was Baillie's birthplace and Shelley's home with the Baxter family from June 1812 through March of 1814. Baillie, whose earliest plays were published in 1798, was in her fifties at the time. In April of 1800, Baillie's highly capable Gothic drama, *De Monfort* (1798), was performed for eight nights at Drury Lane and enjoyed later revivals, one of them again at Drury Lane in 1821 with the protagonist De Monfort played by Kean. Baillie's Marquis De Monfort is a type of the Romantic Hamlet, part Shakespeare and. part Byron. Like Victor Frankenstein, Prince Castruccio, and other heroes in Shelley's novels, he is broodingly introspective. Baillie's stage directions themselves make this quite clear: *"Throwing himself into a chair"* (I.i.237); ...*walks up and down impatiently and irresolute"* (I.ii.248); *"with a disordered air* (II.ii.258); *"lays down his book, and continues in a thoughtful posture"* (II.ii.267). Like Byron's Prisoner of Chillon, Castruccio finds himself alone in a dungeon where he, resembling Baillie's De Monfort, walks up and down waiting "irresolutely, but impatiently, till circumstances should decide the course he was to pursue" (*Valperga* I:226). The Hamlet-like De Monfort is also capable of the inward tempest that Lear and Prospero know so well. "What being...Could in thy breast such horrid tempest wake?" asks his sister about a brother whose vindictiveness toward Rezenvelt has shocked her. Later in the play De Monfort enters a setting that parallels his psychological self: the interior of a dark chapel "of old Gothick architecture" with loud storm-riven winds heard striking the windows and roof (IV.ii.291). De Monfort is in the presence of a newly interred corpse. So like Frankenstein in the graveyard, De Monfort meditates upon death. In *Valperga,* Euthanasia is also placed in a similar dramatic context: when she comes into Lucca after a battle, corpses need to be removed from her path; eventually she observes a garden. The images of which are of death: cypress trees, lizards, and croaking frogs. The garden is a graveyard, and she attempts to engage herself in order philosophically to grapple with the grim facts of mortality:

> Such was the desolate scene which arrested the eyes of Euthanasia, as she looked from her window. "The image of my fortunes," she thought, and turned away, while a tear flowed down her cheek. (II:277)

She too, especially within a passage of quasi-blank verse, is a dramatically Romantic Hamlet.

As in *Valperga, The Last Man* (1826), Shelley's third novel, and her *Perkin Warbeck* (1830), which follows a few years later, treat of the political self. Anne Mellor points out that in Shelley's portrait of Lord Raymond we find "reiterated the judgment on masculine political ambition she had earlier given against Castruccio..." (*The Last Man* x). And like Shelley's penultimate novel *Lodore* (1835), *The Last Man* invokes plays such as *The Winter's Tale* and *The Tempest,* those late Shakespearean romances that unhesitatingly mix tragic, comic, and surreal details to evoke a distant antique land or a new world. Although Adrian, the fictionalized portrait of Percy Shelley, is usually considered the hero of *The Last Man,* it is Lionel Verney who is the first-person narrator and who becomes the last man on the planet. His sister is Perdita, whom Shelley names after Shakespeare's child of both nature and art in *The Winter's Tale.* Like Shakespeare's shepherdess heroine of rural Bohemia, Perdita Verney, as her surname suggests, is associated with the vernal, especially flowers. More than merely part of a pastoral landscape, she possesses an intellect and an imagination that enable her to partake, like her Shakespeare forebear, of artifact and cultivation as well as of nature: "We found her in her flower-adorned alcove; she was reading/the newspaper report of the debate in parliament" (47; added line break). Her brother too is in tune with the vernal as well as the intellectual. In lines that also approach blank verse, Lionel contemplates Birnam Wood and remembers how Malcolm uses nature craftily to defeat Macbeth: "I went by land instead of air, to Dunkeld. The sun was rising as I entered the opening of the hills. After the revolution of ages Birnam hill was again covered with a young forest..." (50).

The Last Man is consciously dramatic throughout. Theatre metaphors abound as do allusions to various Shakespeare texts and characters. In the closing chapters, the three human survivors, Lionel, Clara, and Adrian, inhabit the Villa Pliniana at Torno on Lake Como and then decide to sail from Italy toward Greece seeking other living humans. But a tempest overcomes their modest skiff. In what must have been an emotionally draining and yet therapeutic section of the novel to write, Shelley creates a storm that amplifies, with Romantic force, the sound and the fury of the various Shakespearean tempests. In this way she climactically dramatizes the loss of Clara Everina and Adrian. The autobiographical implications here further charge the narrative with dramatic value (Mellor, *Last Man* ix). In the aftermath of the furious tempest, Lionel becomes all too aware of what it is that now defines him: He has become the last man. As sole human self on earth, Lionel meditates on the world around him. Plague has transformed the entire planet into a human graveyard. A monstrously insidious disease, in other words, has created an apocalyptic monster, the complete devastation of human life. As wandering self, Lionel inhabits a world strewn with the crumbling statues of a myriad of Ozymandiases. Skulls of Yoricks of all races and creeds are everywhere. At one point after coming from Ravenna to Rome to inhabit the Palazzo Colonna, Lionel spends time near the pyramid of Cestius that borders the ultimate

Romantic graveyard, Rome's Protestant Cemetery, the final resting place of John Keats, Percy Shelley, and three-year-old William Shelley. Nature's processes continue, buildings remain standing, animals thrive, but humanity is about to become extinct. Lionel's loved ones are gone, but he observes horses in the fields, and a stray dog befriends him. Implied here is King Lear's powerful realization, as he looks at the corpse of Cordelia, of a grimly obvious fact: "Why should a dog, a horse, a rat, have life, And thou no breath at all?" (V.ii.307-308). Deciding not to take his own life in a statement reminiscent of Hamlet's "O that this too, too sullied flesh" and "To be, or not to be" speeches (337), Lionel chooses a life of wandering. The novel closes as this solitary figure, specifically the brother of the long-lost and hence correctly named Perdita and generally the last member of a human race, prepares his boat for his final voyages. He may not reach an enchanted isle inhabited by Marinas, Imogens, Perditas, and Mirandas, but he does replicate ironically the plight of Prospero when he (alone for no Gonzalo is available to serve him) makes certain that a select number of books is placed aboard. Principal among these books are the works of Shakespeare (342).

Continuing to signal the kinds of dramatic values that interested Shelley are the fifty-eight chapter epigraphs in *The Fortunes of Perkin Warbeck* (1830). Drawn from playwrights such as John Ford, Beaumont, Fletcher, and especially Shakespeare, the epigraphs specify, as do those in her later novel *Lodore* (1835), just how steeped in Elizabethan drama she was. Ford's *Perkin Warbeck* (c. 1625), to be sure, is an important source here. Even more so than Ford's play, Shelley's novel supports the view that Warbeck is indeed the heir apparent Richard of York, the younger of the two princes whom, as shown in Shakespeare's play, Richard III kept prisoner in the Tower. As the supposedly surviving son of Edward IV, Warbeck--who is associated with Flanders and the Netherlands, hence his Dutch name-- claims the throne of Henry VII. Shelley's novel begins where Shakespeare's *Richard III* ends: in 1485 with the Lancastrian defeat of Richard's Yorkist forces at Bosworth Field. Henry VII ascends to the throne, but Warbeck's claim makes the king's reign uneasy. After winning support from other world leaders, including James IV of Scotland whose cousin (Lady Katherine Gordon) Warbeck marries, a showdown battle takes place in Cornwall where Warbeck is captured, imprisoned, and, in 1499, executed. Rife with political themes, the novel is a sweeping, well-researched historical romance in the tradition of Sir Walter Scott, whose advice Shelley sought in its composition.

Exemplifying dramatic substance are two somewhat parallel scenes from Ford's play and Shelley's novel. In Ford, the third and fourth scenes of Act IV are set within the context of Warbeck's strategic departure from Scotland (July of 1497) after the signing of a Scottish-English treaty. His wife Lady Katherine succinctly asserts her attachment to him: "I am your wife;/No human power can or shall divorce/My faith from duty." To which Warbeck responds, "Such another treasure/The earth is bankrupt of" (IV.iii.102-104). Some lines later she reveals her courage to face the whims of fortune: "My fortunes, sir, have armed me to encounter/What chance soe'er they meet with" (127-28). Shelley's Katherine has the same mixture of affection and force, in words that occasionally echo those of Ford's play:

> Katherine looked upon life in a mode very different from the usual one: the luxuries and dignities of the world never in her mind for a moment came in competition with her affections and her duty...her destiny upon earth was to share [Warbeck's] fortunes, and soothe his sorrows...Cleopatra, basking in sunny pomp, borne, the wonder of the world, in her gilded bark, amidst all the aroma of the east, upon the gently-rippling Cydnus, felt neither the pride nor joy of Katherine, as on the poor deck of their dark weather-beaten skiff, she felt pillowed by the downy spirit of love, fanned by its gentle breath. (278)

Both Ford and Shelley owe something to Shakespeare's Cleopatra and other Shakespearean women. The passage above shows a meditative, Hamlet-like Katherine aboard a weather-battered vessel journeying away from her homeland and exploring, quite lyrically, the magical regions of self.

Lodore presents a much different geographical context. It opens in the New World. Shelley's hero, whose relationship with his wife, Lady Lodore, becomes increasingly strained, has gone off to the wilds of North America with Ethel, his young daughter, in self-imposed exile. Shelley indicates at the outset of Chapter 3 through an epigraph from *The Tempest* that Lodore and Ethel are a latter-day Prospero and Miranda. The relationship between father and daughter has been explored, sometimes exasperatingly so, for its possible autobiographical value. Fundamentally, the love between Lodore and Ethel represents a corrective to the incestuous turmoil that occurs in Shelley's novella *Mathilda* and in Percy Shelley's *Cenci.* Unfortunately, the novel suffers a structural blow when the titular hero is killed one quarter of the way into the narrative. Not in the wilderness but in the cultured world of historical New York City, the fictional Lodore participates in a duel that proves disastrous. Ethel returns to England and marries happily. Shelley maintains the Shakespearean aura about her heroine and does so with Romantic flourishes. In Chapter 35, as a rainstorm rages outside Ethel's home, love prompts her to look within and to consider the relevance for her inner life of some lines from *Antony and Cleopatra* and *Othello.* She meditates on the way her mother, Lady Lodore, has foolishly in the past rejected her father. Like "the base Indian," Lady Lodore throws away a pearl, "Richer than all [her] tribe" (35: 145-46). This conscious use of materials from Shakespeare and other Elizabethan or Jacobean playwrights is Shelley's way of building her theatre, developing her dramatic relationships, and drawing inspiration.

In her novels, Shelley displays a sense of drama the power of which is generated by a careful setting out of scene and speech as well as by insight into individual characters and their relationships. Her two verse dramas, more accurately dramatic poetry, do not move beyond the confines of the closet. It is, then, her novels that register a level of dramatic energy impressive enough to assure us that she knew very well how to engage her imagination and put it to work, through her reading, theatregoing, and compositions, in response to a wide array of the dramatic creations of others.

Dramatically, a passage in *The Last Man* recapitulates and simultaneously epitomizes Shelley's theatre. Wandering through a futuristic, twenty-first century London that is slowly being emptied of its population as the plague devastates the planet, the narrator Lionel Verney finds remnants of vibrant life in a persistent, almost deathless, British institution--the theatre:

> I rambled on, oppressed, distracted by painful emotions--suddenly I found myself before Drury Lane Theatre. The play was *Macbeth*--the first actor of the age was there to exert his powers to drug with irreflection the auditors, such a medicine I yearned for, so I entered. The theatre was tolerably well filled. Shakespeare, whose popularity was established by the approval of our centuries, had not lost his influence even at this dread period; but was still "Ut magus," the wizard to rule our hearts and govern our imaginations. (203)

Shelley creates here a sublime irony. We are asked to think of "the first actor of the age" (a descendant of Kean?) as he "struts and frets his [last] hour upon the stage" reciting Macbeth's "To-morrow, and to-morrow, and to-morrow" speech (Vv.19-28). He performs his Macbeth within the context of a deadly reality that is forcing into the grave the collective self that is humanity, which can only creep "from day to day,/To the last syllable of recorded time," hearing, as it crawls toward death and the graveyard, the tempestuous "sound and fury" that may ultimately signify nothing. As is generally the case so many times in Shelley's novels, the literary power here is multiple, the product of fusing the best features of the Romantic drama with the immeasurable resource that is Shakespeare.

Works Cited

Baillie, Joanna. *De Monfort. Seven Gothic Dramas, 1789-1825.* Ed. Jeffrey N. Cox. Athens: Ohio University Press, 1992, 231-314.

Blumberg, Jane. *Mary Shelley's Early Novels.* Iowa City: Iowa University Press, 1993.

Coleridge, Samuel Taylor. *Remorse (1813). The Complete Poetical Works of Samuel Taylor Coleridge.* Ed. Ernest Hartley Coleridge. 2 vols. Oxford: Clarendon Press, 1912.

Cox, Jeffrey N., ed. *Seven Gothic Dramas, 1789-1825.* Athens: Ohio University Press, 1992.

Evans, Bertrand. *Gothic Drama from Walpole to Shelley:* Chapel Hill: University of North Carolina Press, 1947.

Ford, John. *The Chronicle of Perkin Warbeck: A Strange Truth.* The Revels Plays. Ed. Peter Ure. London: Methuen, 1968.

Mellor, Anne K. *Mary Shelley: Her Life, Her Fiction, Her Monsters.* New York: Methuen, 1988.

___. "Introduction" (1993). *The Last Man: Mary Shelley.* Ed. Hugh J. Luke, Jr. Lincoln: University of Nebraska Press, 1965. vii-xxvi.

Nitchie, Elizabeth. *Mary Shelley: Author of Frankenstein.* New Brunswick: Rutgers University Press, 1953.

Otten, Terry. *The Deserted Stage: The Search for Dramatic Form in Nineteenth-Century England.* Athens: Ohio University Press, 1972.

Peake, Richard Brinsley. *Presumption; or, The Fate of Frankenstein (1823). Hideous Progenies: Dramatizations of Frankenstein from the Nineteenth Century to the Present.* Ed. Steven Earl Forry. Philadelphia: University of Pennsylvania Press, 1990. 131-60.

Shakespeare, William. *The Riverside Shakespeare.* Eds. G. Blakemore Evans et. al. Boston: Houghton, 1974.

Shelley, Mary W. *Frankenstein.* Ed. Johanna M. Smith. Boston: St. Martin's, 1992.

___. *Mathilda.The Mary Shelley Reader.* Eds. Betty T. Bennett and Charles E. Robinson. New York: Oxford University Press, 1990. 175-246.

___. *Valperga; or, The Life and Adventures of Castruccio, Prince of Lucca.* 3 vols. London: Whittaker, 1823.

___. *The Last Man.* Ed. Hugh J. Luke, Jr. Lincoln: University of Nebraska Press, 1965.

___. *The Fortunes of Perkin Warbeck.* London: Routledge, 1857.

___. *Lodore.* New York Wallis & Newell, 1835.

Spark, Muriel. *Mary Shelley.* New York: Dutton, 1987.

Sunstein, Emily W. *Mary Shelley: Romance and Reality.* Boston: Little, Brown, 1989.

Mary Shelley and the Romance of Science

Ann Engar

Scientists, to the popular imagination, have always been a breed apart. According to legend, the ancient Greek father of science, Thales of Miletus (fl. 585 B.C.), fell into a pit because he was so busy observing the heavens (Durant 136). This story points to a long held apprehension of scientists as solitary, deep thinkers whose abstruseness often makes them figures of fun. Scientists of the modern period beginning with Galileo Galilei and Francis Bacon have also been satirized in such works as Samuel Butler's *The Elephant in the Moon* and John Gay's *Three Hours After Marriage.* Jonathan Swift attacked the futility of scientific projects sponsored by the Royal Society in his portrayal in Book III of *Gulliver's Travels* of scientists who try to extract sunlight from cucumbers and food from feces.

While figures of fun, scientists, especially after the achievements of Isaac Newton, are also viewed with reverence. Bacon himself earlier portrayed the glorious possibilities of science in *The New Atlantis* (1627), in which a shipwrecked sailor finds an ideal society of scientists working together for practical knowledge to benefit humanity. After Newton, people who penetrate the universe's secrets with their intellect seem like gods. Representing this attitude is Alexander Pope's couplet, "Nature, and Nature's Laws lay hid in Night./God said, Let Newton be! and All was Light" (Butt 808). James Thomson in *Seasons* similarly portrays Newton with his "sage-instructed eye" explaining the colors of the rainbow (*Spring,* 208-12). Other positive, respectful portrayals of science in the eighteenth century include Voltaire's Palace of Science in utopian El Dorado in *Candide.*

Sometimes god-like scientists, however, approach too near the godly in their creations. They violate the boundaries of the human. Like the ancient mythic figure of Daedalus, these humans with beyond-human powers do not foresee the consequences and ramifications of their creations.

As people who push the limits of intellectual achievement, literary scientists encounter more than just experiments that go awry. Figures who work in isolation losing contact with the everyday living risk allowing their intellectual powers to run unchecked into madness. Inge Jonsson finds the origin of *le savant fou* or mad scientists in Aristotle's observation that greatly talented people are disposed to melancholy (in Doorman 160). In modern times, Samuel Johnson's astronomer in *Rasselas* is a mad scientist who notes that his thinking of rain often precedes a shower, which, by cause-effect reasoning, leads him to believe that he controls the weather. Only through the gentle efforts of his friends does he eventually recognize his delusion.

In the nineteenth century, figures of fun recur such as the mermaid-seeking scientist in Thomas Love Peacock's *Nightmare Abbey.* More common, however, is the scientist-as-hero, the isolated, hubristic figure with extraordinary intellectual powers. The two greatest portrayals of scientists in this period are Faust and Frankenstein; no longer secondary characters but men around whom the story revolves. And though with abilities beyond those of other mortals, they are primarily tragic.

Faust and Frankenstein, however, are contrasts. Faust is half sixteenth-century German alchemist and half Romantic rebel His story begins not in an early nineteenth-century laboratory but in a medieval study. He does no experiments but turns to books, magic, and spirits, seeking not knowledge, but mystical, sublime experience. The superhuman deeds he performs or shares in are accomplished through Mephistopheles' magic--the alcohol from the table in the beer cellar--or are engineering feats--the draining of swampland--not the discovery of the laws governing the universe or outright creation

The sources for Mary Shelley's knowledge of science include her father William Godwin's writings, her journals, and Percy Bysshe Shelley's writings. Though Godwin did not follow the plan of his deceased wife Mary Wollstonecraft in giving equal educational opportunities to the males and females of his family, his home was a center of intellectual activity. Godwin was acquainted with Erasmus Darwin, and Humphry Davy, for example, visited (Marshall 264; Mellor 11).

More important, however, was the influence of Percy Shelley, who engaged in scientific experiments at Eton and Oxford. He describes his early passion for "ancient books of Chemistry" (Mellor 18). In their early years together, Mary bought Percy a telescope for his birthday, launched a balloon with him; listened to an explanation of Dr. Gall's system of phrenology, and attended a lecture on electricity, gases, and optical illusions given by Garnerin, one of the pioneers of flight (*Journals* 26, 56, 121, 123). At the time of the writing of *Frankenstein*, they lived close to Lord Byron and his physician Dr. John Polidori, a recent University of Edinburgh graduate. In her 1831 preface to *Frankenstein* she explains that Shelley and Byron have discussed the animation of vermicelli, which sparks her thinking about bringing inanimate forms to life:

> They talked of the experiments of Dr. Darwin, (I speak not of what the Doctor really did, or said that he did, but, as more to my purpose, of what was then spoken of as having been done by him,) who preserved a piece of vermicelli in a glass case, till by some extraordinary means it began to move with voluntary motion. Not thus, after all, would life be given. Perhaps a corpse would be re-animated; galvanism had given token of such things: perhaps the component parts of a creature might be manufactured, brought together, and endued with vital warmth. (*Frankenstein 22*)

"Galvanism" derives from Luigi Galvani, who, as well as Xavier Bichat, Joseph Priestley, and Galvani's nephew Giovanni Aldini, conducted electrical experiments on living and dead animals and plants (Vasbinder 29). This passage exhibits knowledge of their experiments and a careful discrimination among the actual work of scientists, their claims, and the popular talk about them.

Also, Shelley seems to have studied science while writing her story. Besides travel books (which may have inspired Walton's search for a northern passage in *Frankenstein)*, in 1814, she reads William Smellie's *The Philosophy of Natural History* (*Journals* 39). The only other science text in her journal in 1814 through early 1817 appears just as she is writing *Frankenstein:* what she calls "Introduction to Sir H. Davy's Chemistry." Samuel Holmes Vasbinder assumes this is Davy's *Elements of Chemistry,* but Anne Mellor's supposition that it is a pamphlet based on Davy's lectures, *A Discourse, Introductory to a Course of Lectures on Chemistry* (1802), is more probable (91).

Shelley begins Davy's text on October 28, 1816: "Read Introduction to Sir H. Davy's Chemistry--write." In the evening she reads much different fare: Lord George Anson's *A Voyage round the World* and Quintius Curtius's *Life of Alexander.* The next day she reads Davy along with Percy--perhaps for further explanation of some of the concepts. She reads Davy again on October 30 and November 2 while writing during the day and reads other books in the evening. She lists "Introduction to Davy's Chemistry" as her completed reading in 1816. By December 4, she writes to Percy that she has finished writing Chapter 4 of *Frankenstein,* on Frankenstein's discovery of the processes of generating life. She never reads any more Davy (*Journals* 96, 142-44, 148).

Davy's description of what scientists do matches Shelley's: chemists can convert "dead matter into living matter by vegetable organs." But Davy celebrates the abilities of chemists without criticism; science has enabled the chemist to "modify and change the beings surrounding him, and by his experiments to interrogate nature with power, not simply as a scholar, passive and seeking only to understand her operations, but rather as master, active with his own instruments" (16). Davy cautions against extreme optimism concerning science's ability to annihilate "labour, disease, and even death" (22). Unlike Shelley, Davy does not subscribe to the mad-scientist image, claiming that scientific endeavor "may destroy diseases of the imagination, owing to too deep a sensibility; and it may attach the affections to objects, permanent, important, and intimately related to the interests of the human species" (26). Thus, she reads Davy's work for its scientific possibilities and not for its image of the scientist.

The next book she reads perhaps in preparation for *Frankenstein* is Locke's *Essay Concerning Human Understanding.* At this point she is about to write about the monster's first experiences and the growth of his mental powers. She spends a month and a half reading it (November 17, 1816 through January 8, 1817) but apparently never finishes because it does not appear on her list of completed books (*Journals* 146-153). Interestingly enough given Victor Frankenstein's lack of parenting skills with his monster, Shelley reads Lord Chesterfield's letters to his son at the same time she reads Locke.[1]

In subsequent years Shelley does not read many scientific texts, though she does read Comte de Buffon's "Theorie de la terre" in his *Histoire naturelle generate et particuliere* after the *Frankenstein* manuscript has been sent to various publishers (*Journals* 174-176). This suggests not a deep knowledge of science or passion for it but a desire for verisimilitude.

Shelley's concern for the quality of her story also leads her to allow her husband to edit it. As Mellor's study of the early manuscript shows, Percy Shelley renders some of the scientific language and description more precise: Frankenstein's "workshop" becomes his "laboratory"; his chemical "machines" become "instruments"; Frankenstein's focus of study expands from "natural philosophy" to "natural philosophy in its general relations." Percy also adds Waldman's statement that modern science is founded on the work of alchemists and the important explanation of Frankenstein's methodology in analyzing "all the minutiae of causation." Furthermore, he focuses on the god-like/hubristic scientist by changing Frankenstein's description of alchemists from seekers of "immortality and wealth" to "immortality and power" (220-222).

The text itself reveals some of Mary Shelley's understanding of science. Vasbinder's study of the text shows her awareness of recent scientific experiments and ideas, though Vasbinder does not distinguish between the original manuscript and Percy Shelley's changes. One of the most important passages revealing Mary Shelley's knowledge of science is Professor Waldman's speech praising the achievements of modern science:

> The modern masters promise very little; they know that metals cannot be transmuted, and that the elixir of life is a chimera. But these philosophers, whose hands seem only made to dabble in dirt, and their eyes to pour over the microscope and or crucible, have indeed performed miracles. They penetrate into the recesses of nature, and shew how she works in her hiding places. They ascend into the heavens, they have discovered how the blood circulates, and the nature of the air we breathe. They have acquired new and almost unlimited powers; they can command the thunders of heaven, mimic the earthquake, and even mock the invisible world with its shadows (51).

Here, Shelley demonstrates her awareness of experiments with balloons, Harvey's discovery of circulation of the blood, Priestley's discovery of oxygen, and, Vasbinder guesses, Robertson's experiments with optics. Vasbinder explains that mocking the "invisible world with its own shadows" is presumably Etienne-Gaspard Robertson's "ghost-making machine" which supposedly summoned up shades of Voltaire, Rousseau, Robespierre, and other famous deceased Frenchmen (71).

From her somewhat limited exposure to science and epistemology, Shelley creates four scientists in *Frankenstein:* Victor Frankenstein's two professors Krempe and Waldman, the explorer Robert Walton, and Victor himself. While Goethe's presentation of academic science in the character of Wagner satirizes the dullness, ambitions, and emptiness of academic scientists, Shelley's professors of science earnestly strive against old science to proceed on solid premises. They are modern scientists who reverence not the past but the provable. They also differ in personality--Shelley thus avoids the stereotypical trap--Krempe is brusque, ugly, and unsociable (his name suggests "cramp") while Waldman is warm and effusive, especially about science's potential. Interestingly enough, they have little contact. Shelley thus early sets up isolated scientists rather than Bacon's academic community.

Waldman's speech on scientific achievements not only tells us about Shelley's knowledge of science but also about her attitude toward scientists and science. First of all, she regards nature as a female force to be respected. Waldman speaks positively--both nature and the achievements of science are described reverently. Shelley seems to approve of discovering natural workings--the heavens, air, and blood circulation. But when she shifts to the "new and almost unlimited powers" of scientists, she is negative. Commanding the thunders of heaven and mimicking the earthquake may mean the destructiveness of cannon and warfare, made deadlier by scientists and engineers. Mocking the "invisible world with its own shadows" also has negative connotations by implying the chicanery of supposed scientists, or it may condemn those who try to cross between life and death.

Mellor explains that for Shelley "'good' science recognizes and respects the sacred procreative lifeforce troped as 'Mother Nature,' whereas 'bad' science construes nature as dead matter or a machine to be manipulated, controlled and changed" (215). Good science is accurate description; bad science is hubristic manipulation (89). Shelley's criticism of mechanical interference by scientists thus links her with Blake, who holds Newton, Bacon, and Locke responsible for a mechanistic prison of the universe.

Nevertheless, Shelley does not condemn science altogether, does not simply warn that science threatens humanity, does not disparage the ability to master science because of the dangers of science mastering humankind, and does not seek to extinguish the desire to understand the environment. This passage and the positive presentation of Waldman's character suggest a belief that science can lead to important understanding and truth.

Waldman is important not only for his enthusiasm for science but for turning Frankenstein to modern scientific methods. Waldman is a scientist in the Newtonian mold who combines Bacon's empiricism with Descartes's rationalism. He urges Frankenstein to become a true man of science rather than just a "petty experimentalist," to study mathematics and every branch of natural philosophy, not just chemistry

(52). The most sympathetic scientist in the novel, then, is a man excited about the possibilities of science, wide-ranging in inquiry and knowledge, and who reaches out to others with concern about their learning and welfare.

Robert Walton is yet another kind of scientist, outside the academy. What he knows about science comes from his reading, particularly mathematics, medicine, and physical science. For a time he fancied he might become a poet and longed for the immortality of Homer and Shakespeare. When he failed as a poet, he returned to his earlier love of travel. Science appeals to him because of adventure, danger, and glory, what he calls "a love for" and "belief in the marvelous" (30).

Unlike Frankenstein, Walton does not create anything or meddle with nature's basic properties. His goal is to explore the Arctic to see whether the stories told about it are true. He thus begins as a Baconian scientist by testing knowledge empirically. Specifically, he is interested in the North Pole as the source of magnetization, as a spot to observe the heavens, and as a place where a northwest passage may be found.

Walton sees himself as superior to those around him. His ship's master is a generous man who gives the woman who spurns him the means to marry her beloved. Though Walton admires his nobility, he deplores the master's lack of education, his silence, and "ignorant carelessness" (30). He says his own love for the marvelous lifts him out of the "common pathways of men" to places "never before visited." In his dreams he conquers the "untamed yet obedient element" because of his "determined heart and resolved will" (31). He thus represents the optimistic Enlightenment views that humans can achieve whatever they will and that the earth lies open to human scrutiny and dominion.

Like Frankenstein, Walton is driven by his dreams and neglects the needs of those around him. He is determined to press on even when his crew is on the point of mutiny. Finally, though, unlike Frankenstein, Walton does pull back--"I cannot lead them unwillingly to danger, and I must return" (179). In the enclosed society of the ship, he cannot maintain the isolation of a land- and lab-based scientist. Also unlike Frankenstein, he maintains contact with his family: the entire novel is written in the form of letters to his sister.

With all his grand schemes and pride, Walton is not entirely comfortable in a scientist's isolation. Though "the very stars themselves" will witness and testify to his triumph, he needs friends-- someone to participate in his joy and support in dejection (31). This friend he thinks he finds in Frankenstein. When he confides his fondest feelings to Frankenstein--his obsession to the point of sacrificing his fortune and life to his enterprise, his belief that one human life is insignificant compared to the acquisition of knowledge and the "dominion" he is eager to acquire over the elements--Frankenstein recoils in horror, warning Walton that he is verging on madness (35). Frankenstein, then, represents society by warning of the dangers of seeking glory without regard to human life. Friendship thus is an important theme in Shelley's portrayal of modern science: scientists need friends to stay sane and humane.

As a young man, Victor Frankenstein is capable of "intense application" and thirsts for knowledge (42). He delights in probing causes beneath outward appearances. He desires to learn the "secrets of heaven and earth," both "outward substance" and "inner spirit" (43); Insufficiently corrected by his father, he read Cornelius Agrippa, Paraceisus, and Albertus Magnus, assuming their desires for superhuman abilities (immortality and power), a feeling he calls the "fatal impulse" which leads to his ruin.

At this point Frankenstein seems very Faustian; yet, as he narrates the story of his childhood, he likens himself to a story told about Newton (44). When he sees an oak tree blasted by lightning and hears a researcher explain electricity and galvanism, he is thrown into Faustian despair and puts aside his pseudoscientific studies.

When Frankenstein goes to the University of Ingolstadt, his professors dismiss the study of alchemy he has done and inculcate in him the methods of new science. But he never loses his early desire for immortality and power. Though he tenderly describes his family and friends to Walton, at school Frankenstein neglects to write and for long periods of time does not even think of his beloved fiancee Elizabeth.

Frankenstein's interest in the generation of life leads him to charnel houses and slaughterhouses for the material for his monster; and, over a nine-month period, he makes careful lab notes (so that his experiment can be repeated) as he creates his disunified creature. Frankenstein is a thorough materialist and creates without calling on the supernatural. But he also indicates that his purpose is to become a god: "A new species would bless me as its creator and source; many happy and excellent natures would owe their being to me. No father could claim the gratitude of his child so completely as I should deserve theirs" (55). He never considers what his creature's life will be like and whether it wants to live. Later, he says, "I trod heaven in my thought, now exulting in my powers, now burning with the idea of their effects" (176). These effects are his glory, not the creature's needs and actions.

Frankenstein is not equal to fatherhood or godhood. Rather than caring for his creation, he allows it to escape, does not follow it, and lapses into a nervous breakdown. As Vasbinder notes, Frankenstein's language changes from the detached, objective diction of a scientist into the highly charged language of superstition (72-73). He calls his creature such things as "daemon," "filthy fiend," and "my vampire" (55). His problem is the twofold one typical of scientists in popular portrayal: he has focused so much on the creation of his being that he has not considered the aftermath of creation. Working in isolation, he has no one to help.

The importance of friendship becomes clear when Henry Clerval rescues Frankenstein from madness and restores him to health. Henry, like Victor, is ambitious, wanting to be one of the "gallant and adventurous benefactors of our species." But unlike Victor, he keeps in mind the "moral relations of things" (43). According to Victor, Clerval "called forth the better feelings of my heart; he again taught me to love the aspect of nature." He tells Clerval, "A selfish pursuit had cramped and narrowed me, until your gentleness and affection warmed and opened my senses" (68). In following his scientific pursuits, Frankenstein has closed himself off from the essentials of life for a Romantic: the feelings of the heart, love of nature, and use of all the facilities, not just mental.

Though Frankenstein cherishes "the tenderness of friendship" and the beauties of nature, they cannot permanently relieve him once he finds his monster has killed his brother (86). As with Wordsworth, "some turn in the road, some new object suddenly perceived and recognized, reminded me of days gone by, and were associated with the light" (87). He finds this comfort in "maternal nature." But these moments are brief.

Frankenstein, in sympathy for the creature's desire for a mate and willingness thereby to abjure violence, begins his work but this time avoids his previous problems. He takes Clerval along with him. Though he knows Clerval's presence will interfere with his needed solitude, he recognizes that the companionship will preclude "hours of lonely, maddening reflection" and may also keep the monster from intruding on his work.

This time, too, Frankenstein considers the possible consequences of his creation. He realizes that the female will not be bound to the male's promise, that she might reject the male entirely, or that the two of them might form a dynamo to destroy the human race. Frankenstein again worries about his reputation: "I shuddered to think that future ages might curse me as their pest, whose selfishness had not hesitated to buy its own peace at the price, perhaps, of the existence of the whole human race" (141). He rips the female creature apart.

Frankenstein has not, however, lost his pride or the blindness resulting from it. He never suspects the monster will pursue Elizabeth, whom he leaves unprotected. Even after, he does not take responsibility for his own blindness: he blames the monster and associates him with magic. He never asks himself if the creature might have been different if treated differently.

Frankenstein thus is a modern scientist who questions earlier authority, conducts empirical observations, and uses a step-by-step process which can be replicated. He is not a figure of fun nor a confident, rational, god-like creature. Instead, he is plagued by doubt and inaction and is no longer certain of the benefits of his discovery. He needs to listen to his heart and feel the mystery of nature. Most different from earlier portrayals of the scientists is the destructive capacity of his creation. Swift's scientists' cucumbers did not contain a new virus to wipe out the human race, nor could Johnson's astronomer create a nuclear winter to cause all life on earth to wither and die. But Frankenstein's monster easily murders several people and, united with a similarly powerful mate, could populate the world and extinguish the human race.

Scientists this century have become the tragic figures of Frankenstein haunted by the immense powers of their creation. Shelley suggests a means of remediating this problem: scientists must maintain their ties with community and keep human needs paramount notwithstanding their objective studies. They must be willing to become social activists as Frankenstein does in destroying the female and trying to contain the male. This social activism is the role envisioned for scientists in twentieth-century works such as Bertolt Brecht's *Life of Galileo* and Friedrich Durrenmatt's *The Physicists*. As Einstein writes:

> By painful experience we have learned that rational thinking does not suffice to solve the problems of our social life. Penetrating research and keen scientific work have often had tragic implications for mankind...(152)

This is the message of Shelley's scientist.

But no bodily pain could subdue Philip; disgrace and' suffering only
rendered him furious and desperate; and he was considered mutinous and
ungovernable to such a degree, that he passed the first three months of a
seafaring life in a succession of confinement and punishment. (22)

In a futile act of revenge, Philip strikes Lord Robert, his superior and
officer, and consequently faces severe discipline at the first port of call.

But perverse chance redirects both men toward redemption. Chased
by French ships, the *Diomede* is left crippled and without vital supplies,
"little better than a wreck on the mid ocean" (26). A failed attempt to
secure help strands the two rivals upon an island they name "Probation"
(109), where Lord Robert and Philip endure hardship, sickness, and
spiritual pain but find brotherhood. Castaway, Lord Robert dicovers his
vulnerability. The lower orders always clothed him, fed him, and
provided him with the material means of survival. Philip finds the
tables have turned, for on the island his practical knowledge allows him
to build a comfortable camp and to gather nourishment. His physical
strength protects him from the equatorial sun, while Lord Robert, too
proud to ask Philip's pardon, weakens in the bare shelter of rocks.
Consumed by a tropical fever, Lord Robert suffers a spiritual crisis:

Like too many of the young and thoughtless, if he were not profane, he
was careless in matters of religion; in this awful moment, a thousand
instances of neglect and offence against his Creator occurred to his mind,
and he felt that he would have given worlds, had he possessed them, for a
few hours of the time he had so often abused. (73)

Upon discovering his critically ill oppressor, Philip, too, experiences a
crisis of conscience. Empathizing with Lord Robert's mother, Philip
cries out, "wretch that I am! I see her darling son, through the criminal
indulgence of my resentful feelings toward him, reduced to a state so
deplorable, that, if his fond mother could behold him, the sight would
kill her" (79). Thus corrected, Lord Robert and Philip, through illness
and recovery, heal spiritually. "If you repent of your offenses as much
as I have done of my trespasses against you," Philip echoes the Lord's
Prayer, "'we may both be in future more acceptable in the eyes of our
Heavenly Father, to whom hatred, malice, and all uncharitableness, are
most offensive'" (88).

Until rescue, the new friends share labor, teach each other skills, and
live a life of "just...thinking, and noble independence" (95). Social
hierarchy no longer impedes them, though Lord Robert teaches Philip
"higher branches of knowledge" and social manners befitting a

gentleman's calling (101). In the process, Philip, weaned from his lower-class origins, fears he will return to society an outcast; his gentleman's education has permanently altered him. Rescue, he suddenly realizes, would separate the friends forever, for the wider world has not changed. Strickland, then, provides a fairy-tale ending, but one possible within the social flexibility of the British Navy. Her former rivals are rescued, and through Lord Robert's influence, Philip rises to the rank of midshipman. *The Rival Crusoes* concludes optimistically. Personal spiritual recovery leads to public social stability; reclaiming God's grace allows a poor boy to advance professionally and permits a rich boy to delight in "the possession of power, when the influence which more or less it holds in society is applied to a noble purpose" (129).

Barbara Hofland's *The Young Crusoe* presents a less sanguine view of human progress. *The Young Crusoe* depicts a world fickle and dangerously delusive. Misfortune vexes her young hero, thirteen year-old Charles Crusoe, testing his spiritual resolve to the limit. In the process, Charles's sensitivity and piety are quickened, reflecting the growing emphasis upon sentiment, religious fervor, and the soul characteristic of writers more ardently Evangelical than Strickland (Cutt 20). Hofland's novel also mirrors a growing interest in colonial enterprises (Strickland's tale is set back during the American Revolution), in the conflation of missionary and capitalistic goals. *The Young Crusoe* is an allegory of both Christian redemption and imperial reclamation. Charles Crusoe, the only son of a Bombay merchant, is shipwrecked in the Indian Ocean while en route to England. His father and servant (predictably named Sambo) escape his fate and are left to organize a search-and-rescue party at Cape Town. Hofland's main premise, expanded by Victorian boys'-book writers, is that a British boy, armed with his Bible and his culture, can survive any ordeal. Completely isolated, with no adult guidance except what memory provides, Charles must fight depression, illness, and doubt. The only encouragement comes from a parrot, who chides him: "'Don't be a child, don't be a child'" (52) or "'Don't despair, my boy'" (73).

In the opening chapter, Charles imagines being Robinson Crusoe, captivated by the romance of adventure and the illusion of omnipotence. Being castaway puts a new perspective on these fantasies, revealed as vain and unholy:

> "I was then a very wicked, silly boy: I did not know my obligations to
> my dear parents, nor our servants, nor even the people among whom I
> loved, since every creature I knew, more or less, contributed to my safety

and happiness. I am now punished for my ingratitude and folly. I am left to pine away my life in solitude, to die at last of hunger, without one kind voice to cheer me." (53)

With this stark admission, Charles begins life anew. Constantly recalling his father's advice, he abjures idleness, resolving "to give himself continual employment"(57). He portions his day into certain hours for studies and entertainments and organizes his physical life, though Hofland makes clear that spiritual duties take precedence. Charles assiduously studies his Bible, even makes a church, "in which I will keep Sunday" (59). Hofland assails her hero with repeated crises. A monstrous shark (a mainstay of later boys'-book Robinsonnades), as well as a snake den, threatens him--evil creatures lurk in the sea and slither on the land. In response, Charles reads his Bible and rallies his spirits around work or exploring:

> Terrible as his situation would have appeared to his mother, Charles himself was sensible of many comforts; and most devoutly thanked his heavenly Father for the shelter and food which be was blessed with, and the pleasure he experienced in having his poor parrot to speak to, and his lamp to warm his food, and cheer his dark dwelling. (68-69)

But repeated sightings of ships off his island throw Charles into deeper despair; his few pleasures and comforts cannot replace a desired rescue. The elusive ships, unresponsive to his white rescue flag, force "all the evils of his situation...to his mind" (112). He imagines the worst possible end; perhaps his father has forgotten him, or perhaps his father has died. "No, his fate was evident. He must die in this solitude, or venture out in the boat, and perish at sea; for how little, how *very* little chance had he of being seen and taken up in this wide ocean!" (85).

The Young Crusoe emphasizes Charles's conscience. Though action--fending off beasts, enduring storms, sailing his small boat, maintaining his signal--paces the narrative, crises of conscience render the climaxes, and the novel does not build to a final rescue. Hofland constantly reminds us of the thin line dividing life and death, salvation and damnation. Life on a desert island emblematically dramatizes all human life, from childhood on; we are all assailed, she suggests, we are all stranded, unless we accept the shelter of Christian principles. Patricia Demers relates:

> For the Romantic Evangelicals, Christian hope and fortitude, as opposed to any stylized lassitude or despondency, remain uppermost. Their seeing into the life of things is, without contradiction or irony,

simultaneously domestic and eschatological. Their characters' zeal in finding and defining an earthly home prompts their almost automatic longing for a heavenly home. (131)

Once Charles determines to use all his energy to effect rescue--to return to his earthly home, England--his spiritual salvation is assured. Thanking God once more for his deliverance, Charles renounces unmanly despair and pushes forward. Though ships tease him with their nearness, though reminded of his desolation, through activity "he would attain sufficient composure to read, and think on the subject before him, and finally, to pray devoutly, and sleep comfortably" (124).

Rescue equates with spiritual deliverance for both father and son. To this end, Hofland de-emphasizes Charles's physical rescue, using the final section of her narrative to highlight Mr. Crusoe's parallel ordeal. The narrator directs our attention to the father's spiritual and emotional perseverance as he faces the possible loss of a child "under the most afflictive circumstances that he thought possible for a father to endure" (132). Lashed by doubt and uncertainty, Mr. Crusoe weighs the advice of a fellow merchant, Mr. Palmer, who presses him to return to his wife and daughter in England. In a decision like that of Christ's despair on the cross, Mr. Crusoe--emblematic of God the Father--refuses to "forsake" his son (155). Mr. Palmer, an inveterate naysayer, argues that a boy "enervated" by "eastern manner and eastern luxuries...weakening his body" can never survive (158-59). But Hofland's Evangelism stresses the essential moral and spiritual superiority of the mercantile, imperial class. Both father and son survive their crises because spirit conquers the physical--exactly the moral force required in converting others to Christian and capitalistic systems.

Indeed, Hofland's Robinsonnade is the first to stress muscular Christianity, a primary attribute of missionary fiction that furthered British interests abroad. While Mrs. Crusoe and Emily passively await news in England, Mr. Crusoe and Charles enact juxtaposed masculine dramas, the personal dimensions of which reflect the larger historical unfurling of empire.

Ann Fraser Tytler's *Leila; or The Island* also places its protagonists within the context of empire. Similarly, the directives of both earthly and heavenly fathers dominate her story. Though Tytler's is a gentle, at times humorous, account of shipwreck, she shares Hofland's urgency about self-correction and spiritual salvation. As Nancy Cutt explains, Evangelical writers' "basic tenet was that education must subserve religion and be directed to preparation for the after-life. They claimed emphatically that the degree of human happiness was in direct proportion to the degree of submission to the divine Will" (9). Tytler's island, like Hofland's, becomes a spiritual classroom where children learn to submit to religion gladly and to accept parental guidance wholeheartedly. Leila Howard, like Charles Crusoe, must bend to her father's/Father's designs. Island life, then, embodies the filiative order Leila--and by extension young readers--must embrace: God centers creation, one's father centers family life, and gender determines one's fixed role in this naturalized paradigm.

Tytler's Robinsonnade, mirroring Wyss's *Der Schweitzerische Robinson*, does not isolate its heroine from parental authority. Continually, the motherless Leila must struggle against a willfulness that threatens her father's dominion and subverts her nurse's control. Though compassionate, Mr. Howard regards discipline as necessary to salvation:

> "I am sorry to be obliged to punish you, my child; but it is my duty to endeavour in every way to check this impatience of temper, which may lead you into the most frightful faults. You had but just risen from your knees, Leila, where you had been asking your God and Father to love you as his child, to put his Holy Spirit into your heart, and to make you more obedient, more meek and lowly like himself, and fitted to be a lamb of his flock." (77)

Mr. Howard arranges island life to increase his daughter's self-control; her feelings must be channeled toward spiritual and domestic harmony. Her existence follows a quiet routine, relative inaction within the confines of the sheltered cave. Indeed, little adventure interrupts the castaways' lives. "'Here,'" announces Mr. Howard, "'we are cast upon this pleasant land, where there are no wild beasts to devour us, no venomous serpents to make us afraid. A table has been richly furnished for us in the wilderness'"(154). Mr. Howard salvages just enough from the ship to make life agreeable; he never labors exhaustively tilling fields or building an outpost for civilization.

Tytler's Robinsonnade, like the other two, is neither a blueprint for survival nor a chronicle of mastery and dominion over brute nature. It is, instead, a loosely structured, extended dialogue between an all-knowing father and his, young daughter with few dramatic high points and only a perfunctory rescue. The novel celebrates not "the imaginary delights of a *desert* island" (de la Mare 154), but the ecstasy of spiritual awakening. With its emphasis on discipline, vital religion, self-improvement, and duty, *Leila, or The Island* marks the ascendancy of the Evangelical adventure story and bridges Romantic and Victorian children's literature.

It is no exaggeration to say that Leila brings sin to the island. Of herself, Leila confesses, "'Papa, it makes me frightened sometimes when I think how great God is, for you know I am not good'" (71). Mr. Howard assures her, "No human being is perfect in the sight of God; he will forgive our burdensome sins, "For like as a father pitieth his own children, even so is the Lord merciful unto them that fear him" (72). Yet for Leila, the island becomes a metaphysical battleground on which every sin falls exposed to God. Tytler's narrative is punctuated by Leilas confessions, marking her evolution as a Christian. Though life at times provokes Leila's sins, it also reinforces other behavior pleasing to her earthly--and by implication heavenly--father. She determines, with her nurse, to improve her cooking and her husbandry. She also transforms herself into an agreeable companion, eagerly learning theology, zoology, and botany. Her domestic growth, however, is overshadowed by the spiritual. Island life increases her love of God: "I say to myself that God is very good to have made this island so beautiful for us; and when you are kissing me, and looking at me so kindly, then I love God more for keeping you alive to kiss me...I read the Bible a great deal more now" (88). God's and Mr. Howard's wills mute her own.

Reflecting Evangelical division of gender, Tytler uses adventure to socialize young females (Vallone 80). The narrative's passivity, its emphases on submission and curtailment, posit a different reality from that constructed in later boys' books. Here is not what Jacqueline Rose characterizes as "the opposition which stakes out its territory against the rest" (84), but the opposition (Leila) that relinquishes its territory for the rest. As Vallone asserts, in Evangelical texts "feminine passion...is to be feared and avoided as a disruption of domestic tranquility...Conquering anger and aggression is certainly a religious tenet...but it is also a conduct book imperative for girls" (86-87).

The pivotal moment in Leila's development occurs, stereotypically, after a violent storm. Her father carries home a near-drowned girl from a shipwreck, who dies in Leila's bed. Overwhelmed, Leila clasps the corpse so tightly she swoons. To abate her passion, Mr. Howard gently remonstrates, "let me see you bow in meek submission to His will" (206). Death sobers Leila, as does her father's subsequent battle with fever. "Her extreme childishness had passed away" (219). She is now ready to accept "meek submission," to shape herself according to filial dictates. Having crossed this threshold, Leila's island education completes itself, and Tytler provides a convenient rescue ship and passage home to England.

Robinson Crusoe itself underwent abridgment and reinterpretation in the nineteenth century. One high-minded, anonymous Evangelical editor declares,

> It blends instruction with amusement in a way no other production of human intellect has ever succeeded in doing. While depicting a solitary individual struggling against misfortune, it indicates the justice and mercy of Providence; and while inculcating the duty of self-help, asserts the complete dependence of man upon a higher power for all he stands in need of. ("Preface" xii)

Though Martin Green argues "[this] evangelical strain of course goes against the grain of the Robinson story itself, with its upward curve of adventure, optimism, and expectation" (80), Evangelical writers appropriate the Robinsonnade expressly to rechannel children's "upward curve" toward spiritual renewal. Fiction like *The Rival Crusoes, The Young Crusoe,* and *Leila; or The Island* temper adventure, conducting its imaginative reaches toward conduct books and domestic fiction. These writers are among a group that "[drew] strength from the underworld adventure story invented by Defoe, and the more ancient pattern of romance" yet convert that strength into moral, religious tales of immense popularity (Bratton 66). By positing firm parallels among the domestic, the political, and the divine, these works prefigure Victorian adventure tales, which further adventure's promotion of social order, imperial politics, and missionary objectives. The Romantic era, then, encouraged a vital shift in British children's fiction, the accommodation of secular desires to spiritual demands.

Works Cited

Anonymous. "Preface." *The Life and Strange Adventures of Robinson Crusoe of York, Mariner.* London: Cassell, 1869.

Bratton, J.S. *The Impact of Victorian Children's Fiction.* London: Croom, 1981.

Coleridge, Samuel Taylor. "Defoe." *Coleridge: Selected Poetry and Prose.* Ed. Stephen Potter. London: Nonesuch, 1962.

Cutt, Nancy. *Ministering Angels: A Study of Nineteenth-Century Evangelical Writing for* Children. Broxbourne: Five Owls Press, 1979.

Darton, F. J. Harvey, *Children's Books in England: Five Centuries of Social Life.* 3rd ed. Cambridge: Cambridge University Press, 1982.

de la Mare, Walter. *Desert Islands.* London: Faber, 1930.

Demers, Patricia. "Mrs. Sherwood and Hesba Stratton: The Letter and the Spirit
      of Evangelical Writing of and for Children." *Romanticism and
      Children's Literature in Nineteenth-Century England.* Ed. James Holt
      McGavran, Jr. Athens: University of Georgia Press, 1991. 129-149.
Edgeworth, Richard Lovell and Maria. *Practical Education.* Vol. 1. 1798;
      Boston: T.B. Wait, 1815.
Green, Martin. *The Robinson Crusoe Story.* University Park: Pennsylvania
      State University Press, 1990.
Hofland, Barbara. *The Young Crusoe, or the Shipwrecked Boy.* Boys and Girls
      Library 12. 1828; rpt. New York. Harper, 1833.
Jackson, Mary V. *Engines of Instruction, Mischief, and Magic. Children's
      Literature in England from Its Beginnings to 1839.* Lincoln:
      University of Nebraska Press, 1989.
Pickering, Samuel F., Jr. *Moral Instruction and Fiction for Children, 1749-
      1820.* Athens: University of Georgia Press, 1993.
Rose, Jacqueline. *The Case of Peter Pan, of the Impossibility of Children's
      Fiction.* London: Macmillan, 1984.
Said, Edward. *The World, the Text the Critic.* Cambridge: Harvard University
      Press, 1979.
Strickland, Agnes. *The Rival Crusoes, or The Shipwreck.* 2nd. ed. London:
      Harris, 1826.
Summerfield, Geoffrey. *Fantasy and Reason: Children's Literature in the
      Eighteenth Century.* Athens: University of Georgia Press, 1984.
Tytler, Ann Fraser. *Leila; or, The Island.* 1833; New York, Francis, 1853.
Vallone, Lynn. "'A humble Spirit under Correction!': Tracts, Hymns and the
      Ideology of Evangelical Fiction for Children, 1780-1820." *The Lion
      and the Unicorn.* 15.2 (1991): 72-95.

Representative Chronology of English Novels by Women of the Romantic Period[1]

1783	*Two Mentors* by Clara Reeve
1783-85	*The Recess* by Sophia Lee
1785	*Anna, or the Memoirs of a Welch Heiress, Interspersed with Anecdotes of a Nabob* by Agnes Maria Bennett
	Maria by Elizabeth Blower
	The Conquests of the Heart by Elizabeth Sophia Tomlins
1786	*The Balloon, or Aerostatic Spy* by Miss Ballin
	Juvenile Indiscretions by Agnes Maria Bennett
	Moreton Abbey, or The Fatal Mystery by Harriet Chilcot
	The Convent, or the History of Sophia Nelson by Anne Fuller
	The Errors of Innocence by Harriet Lee
	Warbeck by Sophia Lee
	The Gamesters by Anna Maria Mackenzie
1787	*Ela, or the Delusions of the Heart* by Mrs. Burke
	The Adventures of Jonathan Corncob, Loyal American Refugee, Written by Himself by Maria Susanna Cooper
	Elfrida or Paternal Ambition by Maria Edgeworth-
	Alan Fitz-Osborne, an Historical Tale by Anne Fuller
	Louisa; or The Cottage on the Moor by Elizabeth Helme
	History of Miss Greville by Mrs. James Keir
	The Romance of Real Life by Charlotte Smith
	Victim of Fancy by Elizabeth Sophia Tomlins
1788	*Helena* by a Lady of Distinction
	Features from Life, or a Summer Visit by Elizabeth Blower
	The Niece, or the History of Sukey Thornby by Mrs. P. Gibbes
	Clara and Emmeline by Elizabeth Helme

Emmeline, or the Orphan of the Castle by Charlotte
　　Smith
Memoirs of the Miss Holmsbys by Sarah Emma Spencer
Mary, A Fiction by Mary Wollstonecraft

1789　*Agnes de Couri, A Domestic Tale* by Agnes Maria Bennett
Darnley Vale, or Emelia Fitzroy by Elizabeth Bonhote
The Castles of Athlin and Dunbayne by Ann Radcliffe
The Vicar of Landsdowne by Regina Maria Roche
Ethelinde by Charlotte Smith

1790　*Statue Room, an Historical Tale* by Miss Ballin
The Citizen by Mrs. Gomersall of Leeds
Dinarbas by Ellis Cornelia Knight
Euphemia by Charlotte Lennox
The Dangers of Coquetry by Amelia Opie
The History of Miss Meredith by Eliza Parsons
A Sicilian Romance by Ann Radcliffe
The Philanthropic Rambler by Jane Timbury
Julia by Helen Maria Williams

1791　*A Simple Story* by Elizabeth Inchbald
The Romance of the Forest by Ann Radcliffe
The School for Widows by Clara Reeve
Celestina by Charlotte Smith

1792　*Marcus Flaminius, or a View of the Military, Political
　　　and Social Life of the Romans* by Ellis Cornelia
　　　Knight
The Errors of Education by Eliza Parsons
Vancenza, or The Dangers of Credulity by Mary
　　Robinson
Desmond by Charlotte Smith
Memoirs of a Baroness by Elizabeth Sophia Tomlin

1793　*Ellen, Countess of Castel Howel* by Agnes Maria Bennett
Anecdotes of the Delborough Family by Susannah
　　Minifie
Memoirs of Mary by Susannah Minifie
Castle of Wolfenbach by Eliza Parsons
Ellen and Julia by Eliza Parsons
*Woman as She Should Be, or the Memoirs of Mrs.
　　Menville* by Eliza Parsons
Sir Roger de Clarendon by Clara Reeve
The Maid of Hamlet by Regina Maria Roche
The Old Manor House by Charlotte Smith
The Recluse of the Appenines by Miss Street
*The Advantages of Education; or The History of Maria
　　Williams* by Jane West

1794	*Duncan and Peggy* by Elizabeth Helme
	Lucy by Eliza Parsons
	The Mysteries of Udolpho by Ann Radcliffe
	The Shrine of Beriha by Mary Robinson
	The Widow, or A Picture of Modern Times by Mary Robinson
	The Banished Man by Charlotte Smith
	The Wanderings of Warwick Charlotte Smith
1795	*The Abbey of Clugny* by Mary Meeke
	The Voluntary Exile by Eliza Parsons
	Mrs. Montalbert by Charlotte Smith
	Royal Captives by Ann Yearsley
1796	*Camilla* by Fanny Burney
	Translation of the Letters of a Hindoo Rajah by Elizabeth Hamilton
	The Memories of Emma Courtney by Mary Hays
	The Ruins of Avondale Priory by Isabella Hedgeland
	The Farmer of Ingelwood Forest by Elizabeth Helme
	Nature and Art by Elizabeth Inchbald
	Delves, A Welsh Tale by Susannah Minifie
	Mysterious Warning by Eliza Parsons
	Women as They Are by Eliza Parsons
	Angelina by Mary Robinson
	The Wanderings of the Imagination by Mary Robinson
	The Children of the Abbey by Regina Maria Roche
	Marchmont by Charlotte Smith
	A Gossip's Story by Jane West
	The History of Ned Evans: Interspersed with Moral and Critical Remarks by Jane West
1797	*The Beggar Girl and her Benefactors* by Agnes Maria Bennett
	Bungay Castle by Elizabeth Bonhote
	Albert, or the Wilds of Strathnavern by Elizabeth Helme
	The Mysterious Wife by Mary Meeke
	Palmira and Ermance by Mary Meeke
	The Girl of the Mountains by Eliza Parsons
	An Old Friend with a New Face by Eliza Parsons
	Walsh Colville, or A Young Man's First Entrance into Life by Anna Maria Porter
	The Italian or the Confessional of the Black Penitents by Ann Radcliffe
	Hubert de Sevrac. a Romance of the 18th Century by Mary Robinson
	Walsingham or the Pupil of Nature by Mary Robinson

The Church of Saint Siffrid by Jane West
1798   *Derwent Priory* by A. Kendall
Vagabond, Waldorf, or the Dangers of Philosophy by
    Sophia King
The Sicilian by Mary Meeke
Anecdotes of Two Well-Known Families by Eliza Parsons
Octavia by Anna Maria Porter
Clermont by Regina Maria Roche
The Young Philosopher by Charlotte Smith
Rosalind de Tracy by Elizabeth Sophia Tomlins
1799   *The Victim of Prejudice* by Mary Hays
Cordelia, or the Romance of Real Life by Sophia King
Ellesmere by Mary Meeke
Harcourt by Mary Meeke
The Valley of St. Gothard by Eliza Parsons
The Spirit of the Elbe by Jane Porter
False Friend by Mary Robinson
The Natural Daughter by Mary Robinson
A Tale of the Times by Jane West
Maria, or The Wrongs of Woman a Posthumous Fragment
    by Mary Wollstonecraft
1800   *De Valcourt* by Agnes Maria Bennett
Castle Rackrent by Maria Edgeworth
Memoirs of Modern Philosophers by Elizabeth Hamilton
Tales of the Abbey by A. Kendall
The Victim of Friendship by Sophia King
Anecdotes of the Altamont Family by Mary Meeke
The Miser and His Family by Eliza Parsons
The Nocturnal Visit by Regina Maria Roche
Eliza by Mrs. Yeates
1801   *Belinda* by Maria Edgeworth
St. Margaret's Grave; or the Nun's Story by Elizabeth
    Helme
The Fatal Secret or the Unknown Warrior by Sophia King
Mysterious Husband by Mary Meeke
Which is the Man? by Mary Meeke
Father and Daughter by Amelia Opie
The Peasant of Ardenne Forest by Eliza Parsons
The Two Princes of Persia by Jane Porter
1802   *Independence* by Mary Meeke
Midnight Weddings by Mary Meeke
The Mysterious Visit by Eliza Parsons
Correlia, or The Mystic Tomb by Sarah Sheriffe
The Infidel Father by Jane West

1803	*St. Clair of the Isles* by Elizabeth Helme
	A Tale of Mystery, or Celina by Mary Meeke
	St. Clair by Sydney Owenson (Lady Morgan)
	Thaddeus of Warsaw by Jane Porter
1804	*Memoirs of the Life of Agrippina, Wife of Germanicus* by Elizabeth Hamilton
	Harry Clinton; or A Tale of Youth by Mary Hays
	The Life of a Lover by Sophia Lee
	Village Anecdotes; or The Journal of a Year, from Sophia To Edward by Elizabeth Le Noir
	Amazement! by Mary Meeke
	Murray House by either Mary Meeke or Eliza Parsons
	The Nine Days' Wonder by Mary Meeke
	The Old Wife and Young Husband by Mary Meeke
	Something Odd by Mary Meeke
	Adeline Mowbray, or the Mother and Daughter by Amelia Opie
	The Lake of Killarney by Anna Maria Porter
	Sketch of the Campaign of Count A Suwarrow Ryminski by Jane Porter
1805	*The Confessions of the Nun of St. Omer* by Charlotte Dacre
	The Modern Griselda by Maria Edgeworth
	Pilgrim of the Cross, or the Chronicles of Christabelle de Mowbray by Elizabeth Helme
	A Description of Latium by Ellis Cornelia Knight
	The Wonder of the Village by Mary Meeke
	The Novice of St. Dominick by Sydney Owenson (Lady Morgan)
	A Sailor's Friendship and a Soldier's Love by Anna Maria Porter
1806	*Vicissitudes Abroad, or The Ghost of My Father* by Agnes Maria Bennett
	Zofloya; or The Moor by Charlotte Dacre
	Leonora by Maria Edgeworth
	Something Strange by Mary Meeke
	The Wild Irish Girl by Sydney Owenson (Lady Morgan)
	The Discarded Son by Regina Maria Roche
1807	*The Libertine* by Charlotte Dacre
	St. Clair, or the Heiress of Desmond by Sydney Owenson (Lady Morgan)
	The Convict; or the Navy Lieutenant by Eliza Parsons
	The Hungarian Brothers by Anna Maria Porter
	Alvondon Vicarage by Regina Maria Roche
1808	*The Cottagers of Glenburnie* by Elizabeth Hamilton

Clara de Montfier by Elizabeth Le Noir
There is a secret, find it out! by Mary Meeke
Coelebs in Search of a Wife by Hannah More
1809   *Ennui* by Maria Edgeworth
The History of an Officer's Widow and Her Young Family
by Barbara Hofland
Laughton Priory by Mary Meeke
Woman, or Ida of Athens by Sydney Owenson (Lady
Morgan)
Don Sebastian, or House of Braganza by Anna Maria
Porter
1810   *Self-Control* by Mary Brunton
The Scottish Chiefs by Jane Porter
The House of Osma and Almerida by Regina Maria Roche
The Refusal by Jane West
1811   *Sense and Sensibility* by Jane Austen
The Passions by Charlotte Dacre
Strategems Defeated by Mary Meeke
The Missionary--An Indian Tale by Sydney Owenson
(Lady Morgan)
1812   *Self-Indulgence, A Tale of the Nineteenth Century* by
Charlotte Bury
The Absentee by Maria Edgeworth
Magdalen; or the Penitent of Godstow by Elizabeth Helme
The Son of a Genius by Barbara Hofland
Matrimony, the height of bliss, or the extreme of misery by
Mary Meeke
Temper by Amelia Opie
The Monastery of St. Colombe by Regina Maria Roche
The Loyalists by Jane West
1813   *Pride and Prejudice* by Jane Austen
Patronage by Maria Edgeworth
Ivanowna or the Maid of Moscow by Barbara Hofland
Patience and Perseverance; or the Modern Griselda by
Barbara Hofland
Trecothic Bower by Regina Maria Roche
1814   *Mansfield Park* by Jane Austen
Thie Wanderer, or Female Difficulties by Fanny Burney
Modern Times; or The Age we live in by Elizabeth Helme
Conscience by Mary Meeke
O'Donnel by Sydney Owenson (Lady Morgan)
The Recluse of Norway by Anna Maria Porter
The Infant's Progress by Mary Martha Sherwood
Alicia de Lacy by Jane West

1815	*Discipline* by Mary Brunton
	A Father as He Should Be by Barbara Hofland
	The Spanish Campaign or The Jew by Mary Meeke
	The Pastor's Fire-Side by Jane Porter
	The Indian Pilgrim by Mary Martha Sherwood
	Little Henry and His Bearer by Mary Martha Sherwood
1816	*Emma* by Jane Austen
	Faith and Fiction; or Shining Lights in a Dark Generation by Agnes Maria Bennett
	The Blind Farmer and His Children by Barbara Hofland
	Glernarvon by Caroline Lamb
	Valentine's Eve by Amelia Opie
1817	*Harrington* by Maria Edgeworth
	Ormond by Maria Edgeworth
	The Knight of St. John by Anna Maria Porter
1818	*Northanger Abbey and Persuasion* by Jane Austen
	Marriage by Susan Ferrier
	Florence McCarthy by Sydney Owenson (Lady Morgan)
	The Fast of St. Magdalen by Anna Maria Porter
	Frankenstein, or the Modern Prometheus by Mary Shelley
	A History of the Fairchild Family, or The Child's Manual by Mary Martha Sherwood
1819	*Emmeline* by Mary Brunton
	The Veiled Protectress, or The Mysterious Mother by Mary Meeke
	The Munster Cottage Boy by Regina Maria Roche
1821	*Theodore, or the Crusaders* by Barbara Hofland
	The Village of Mariendorpt by Anna Maria Porter
1822	*Conduct is Fate* by Charlotte Bury
	Graham Hamilton by Caroline Lamb
	Madeline by Amelia Opic
	Roche-Blanche, or the Hunters of the Pyrenees by Anna Maria Porter
1823	*Adeline; or the Intrepid Daughter* by Barbara Hofland
	Integrity by Barbara Hofland
	Ada Reis by Caroline Lamb
	What Shall Be, Shall Be by Mary Meeke
	Self-Delusion or Adelaide D'Hauteroch by Amelia Opie
	Bridal of Dunnamora, and Lost and Won by Regina Maria Roche
	Valperga, or The Life and Adventures of Castruccio, Prince of Lucca by Mary Shelley
1824	*The Inheritance* by Susan Ferrier

Theresa Marchmont, or the Maid of Honour by
        Catherine Gore
The Negro Boy's Tale by Amelia Opie
*Duke Christian of Luneburg or Traditions of the
        Hartz* by Jane Porter
The Tradition of the Castle by Regina Maria Roche

1825   *The Castle Chapel* by Regina Maria Roche

1826   *De Foix, or Sketches of the Manners and Customs of
        the Fourteenth Century* by Anna Bray
The Black Man's Lament, or How to Make Sugar by
        Amelia Opie
Honor O'Hara by Anna Maria Porter
*Gaston de Blondeville: Or the Court of Henry III
        Keeping Festival in Ardenne* by Ann
        Radcliffe
The Last Man by Mary Shelley
The Rival Crusoes, or The Shipwreck by Agnes
        Strickland

1826-30   *Our Village* by Mary Russell Mitford

1827   *The Lettre de Cachet and The Reign of Terror* by
        Catherine Gore
The O'Briens and the O'Flahertys by Sydney
        Owenson (Lady Morgan)
Ringrove by Jane West
The Protestant. A Tale of The Reign of Queen Mary
        by Anna Bray
The White Hoods by Anna Bray
Flirtation by Charlotte Bury
Contrast by Regina Maria Roche

1830   *Fitz of Fitz-Ford. A Legend of Devon* by Anna Bray
The Talba by Anna Bray
The Exclusives by Charlotte Bury
The Separation by Charlotte Bury
Women as They Are, or Manners of the Day by
        Catherine Gore
The Barony by Anna Maria Porter
The Fortunes of Perkin Warbeck by Mary Shelley

1831   *Destiny or The Chief's Daughter* by Susan Ferrier
Mothers and Daughter's: a Tale of the Year 1830 by
        Catherine Gore
The Tuileries by Catherine Gore
Romance and *Reality* by Letitia Elizabeth Landon

1832   *The Fair of Mayfair* by Catherine Gore
The Opera by Catherine Gore

1833	*The Young Crusoe*, or *the Shipwrecked Boy* by Barbara Hofland
	Sir Guy de Lusignan by Ellis Cornelia Knight
	Leila, or The Island by Ann Tytler
1834	*Warleigh, or The Fatal Oak* by Anna Bray
	The Disinherited and The Ensnared by Charlotte Bury
	Helen by Maria Edgeworth
	The Hamiltons, or the New Era by Catherine Gore
	Pin Money by Catherine Gore
	Francesca Carrera by Letitia Elizabeth Landon
	The Nun's Picture by Regina Maria Roche
1835	*The Devoted* by Charlotte Bury
	King O'Neil or The Irish Brigade by Catherine Gore
	Belford Regis, or Sketches of a Country Town by Mary Russell Mitford
	The Princess, or the Beguine by Sydney Owenson (Lady Morgan)
1836	*Lodore* by Mary Shelley
	The Diary of a Desennuyee by Catherine Gore
	Mrs. Armytage, or Female Domination by Catherine Gore
	Traits and Trials of Early Life by Letitia Elizabeth Landon
1837	*Love* by Charlotte Bray
	Trelawny of Trelawne, or The Prophecy. A Legend of Cornwall by Anna Bray
	.The Divorced by Cbarlotte Bury
	Memoirs of a Peeress, or the Days of Fox by Catherine Gore
	Stokeshill Place or the Man of Business by Catherine Gore
	Ethel Churchill by Letitia Elizabeth Landon
	Falkner by Mary Shelley
1838	*The Heir of Selwood or Three Epochs of a Life* by Catherine Gore
	The Maid of Croissey, or Theresa's Vow by Catherine Gore
	The Rose Fancier's Manual by Catherine Gore
	The Woman of the World by Catherine Gore
1839	*Trials of the Heart* by Anna Bray
	The Cabinet Minister by Catherine Gore
1840	*The History of a Flirt Related by Herself* by Charlotte Bury

The Dowager, or the New School for Scandal by
Catherine Gore
Preferment, or My Uncle the Earl by Catherine Gore

Endnote

[1] My sources sometimes conflicted so I have in those cases gone either with what seemed the more established work's date or title or with the one more frequently appearing.

Selected Bibliography

Ahrends, Gunter, and Hans-Jurgen Diller, eds. *English Romantic Prose.*
Essen: Die Blaue Eule, 1990.

Allen, Walter. *The English Novel. A Short Critical History.* New York: Dutton,
1954.

Armstrong, Nancy. *Desire and Domestic Fiction.* New York: Oxford, 1987.

Blain, Virginia, Patricia Clements, and Isobel Grundy. *The Feminist
Companion to Literature in English. Women Writers from the Middle
Ages to the Present.* New Haven: Yale University Press, 1990.

Church, Richard. *The Growth of the English Novel.* London: Methuen, 1957;
rpt. New York: Barnes & Noble, 1961.

Clayton, Jay. *Romantic Vision and the Novel.* Cambridge: Cambridge
University Press, 1987.

Copley, Stephen, and John Whale, eds *.Beyond Romanticism: New Approaches
to Texts and Contexts 1780-1832.* New York: Routledge, 1992.

Dabundo, Laura, ed. *Encyclopedia of Romanticism: Culture in Britain, 1780s-
1830s.* New York: Garland, 1992.

Ferguson, Moira, ed. *First Feminists: British Women Writers, 1578-1799.*
Bloomington: Indiana University Press and Old Westbury: Feminist
Press, 1985.

Karl, Frederick. *A Reader's Guide to The Nineteenth Century British Novel.*
New York: Noonday, 1967.

Kelly, Gary. *English Fiction of the Romantic Period, 1789-1830.* New York:
Longman, 1989.

Kiely, Robert. *The Romantic Novel in England.* Cambridge: Harvard
University Press, 1973.

Mudge, Bradford K., ed, *British Romantic Novelists, 1789-1832 Dictionary of
Literary Biography.* Detroit: Gale, 1992.

Neill, Diana. *A Short History of the English Novel.* New York: Collier, 1967.

Skilton, David. *The English Novel: Defoe to the Victorians.* London: David
& Charles, 1977.

Spencer, Jane. *The Rise of the Woman Novelist: From Aphra Behn to Jane
Austen.* New York: Basil Blackwell, 1986.

Spender, Dale. *Mothers of the Novel: 100 Good Women Writers Before Jane*

Austen. New York: Pandora, 1986.

Spender, Dale, and Janet Todd, eds. *British Women Writers: An Anthology from the Fourteenth Century to the Present.* New York: Peter Bendrick, 1989.

Stevenson, Lionel. *The English Novel: A Panorama.* Boston: Houghton Mifflin, 1960.

Todd, Janet. *A Dictionary of British American Women Writers, 1660-1800.* Totowa: Rowman & Allanheld, 1985.

Tompkins, J.M.S. *The Popular Novel in England 1770-1800.* London: Constable, 1932; rpt. Lincoln: University of Nebraska Press, 1967.

Watt, Ian. *The Rise of the Novel: Studies in Defoe, Richardson and Fielding.* London: Chatto, 1957; rpt. Berkeley: University of California Press, 1974.

Wilson, Mona. *Jane Austen and Some Contemporaries.* Port Washington: Kennikat Press, 1966.

Writers of the Romantic Period, 1789-1832. Detroit: Gale, 1992.

Index

About the Contributors

Karla Alwes is an Associate Professor of English at the State University College at Cortland. Her book *Imagination Transformed: The Evolution of the Female Character in Keats's Poetry* has been published.

William D. Brewer is Professor of English at Appalachian State University in Boone, North Carolina. He is the author of *The Shelley-Byron Conversation* (University Press of Florida, 1994) and articles in *Papers on Language & Literature, Philological Quarterly, Keats-Shelley Journal, Southern Humanities Review, European Romantic Review*, and other journals. He is also the co-editor of *Mapping Male Sexuality: Nineteenth-Century England* (Fairleigh Dickinson University Press.

Laura Dabundo is on the faculty of Kennesaw State University, where she is Professor and Chair of the English Department. She edited the *Encyclopedia of Romanticism: Culture in Britain, 1780s to 1830s*, and is currently working on a book on Jane Austen.

Ann Engar teaches in the Honors and LEAP programs at the University of Utah, where she is a Presidential Teaching Scholar. She has published numerous articles on women writers, eighteenth century literature and teaching, most recently in *American National Biography*. She is also a senior bibliographer for the Modern Language Association *International Bibliography*.

Angela Esterhammer is Associate Professor of English and Comparative Literature at the University of Western Ontario. She is the author of *Creating States:*

Studies in the Performative Language of John Milton and William Blake (1994), a book of translations from Rainer Maria Rilke, and articles on nineteenth- and twentieth-century literature and linguistic philosophy. Her book *Romanticism and the Performative: Language in Action* is forthcoming from Stanford University Press.

Deborah Kennedy is an Associate Professor in the Department of English at St. Mary's University. She has published on authors such as William Wordsworth, Charlotte Smith, and Felicia Hemans, and she has completed a book-length study entitled *Helen Maria Williams and the Age of Revolution*.

Kathryn Kirkpatrick teaches women's studies and writing at Appalachian State University. She has written articles on Maria Edgeworth and Hannah More and is editing Edgeworth's *Belinda*.

Susan Naramore Maher, Associate Professor of English at the University of Nebraska at Omaha, has published numerous articles on nineteenth-century literature, children's literature, and American regional literature. Long interested in the adventure genre, she plans to complete a book-length study on women writers of adventure. Currently, though, she is at work on a book, *Deep Maps: Literary Cartographies of the Great Plains*, which charts the emergence of regional nature writers in the late twentieth century.

David S. Miall is Associate Professor of English at the University of Alberta and editor of *Humanities and the Computer: New Perspectives*. He directs the biannual Coleridge Summer Conference in Somerset, England.

Vincent F. Petronella, Professor of English, University of Massachusetts Boston, has published several articles on Shakespeare and others; essays in the *Encyclopedia of Romanticism*; and chapters in the MLA volumes on *King Lear* and Shelley. During his five years as President of the Boston Browning Society (founded 1885), Dr. Petronella lectured often on the Brownings in connection with Shakespeare and/or the Shelleys.

Joseph Rosenblum teaches and writes in Greensboro, North Carolina.

John A. Stoler is Professor of English and Associate Dean of the College of Fine Arts and Humanities at the University of Texas-San Antonio. He is the author of *Ann Radcliffe: The Novel of Suspense and Terror, Henry Fielding: An Annotated Bibliography of Modern Criticism, and Daniel Defoe: An Annotated Bibliography of Modern Criticism.* Fielding is the focus of his current research.

Professor David W. Ullrich is Associate Professor of English at Birmingham-Southern College. His scholarly interests are varied and include articles on Coleridge in *The Wordsworth Circle* and Hemingway in *Studies in Short Fiction.* His poetry can be found in *Negative Capability, The Madison Review,* and *Birmingham Poetry Review.* Recently, he has turned his energies to sculpture and has won commissions for large-scale, public sculptures. He thanks his wife, Joanne, and children, Dana and Jack, for their continued support and patience.